Yōkai Girls
6
Funatsu Kazuki

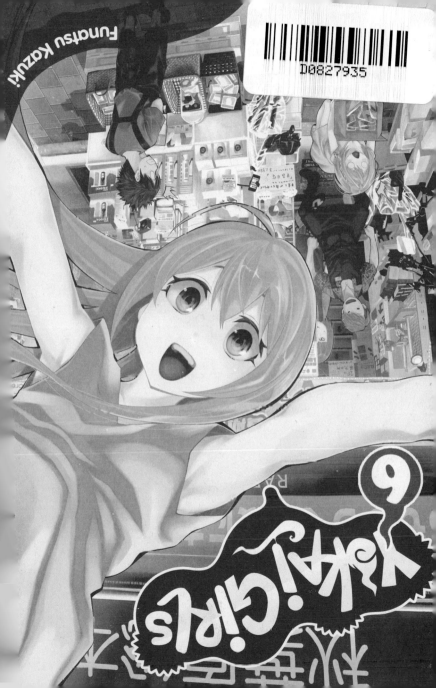

The Cast of Monster Girls!

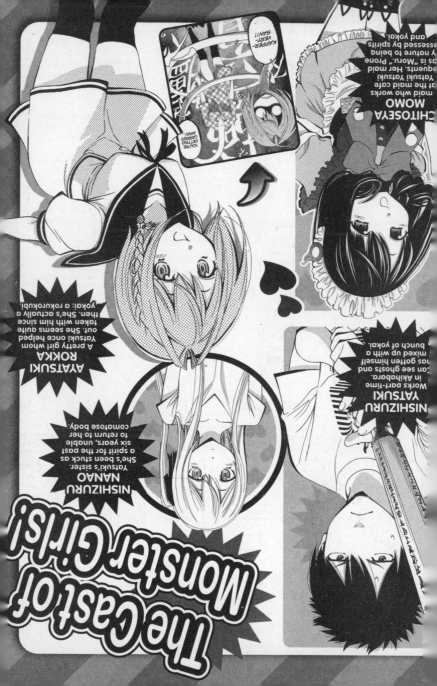

CHITOSEYA MOMO
maid who works at the maid cafe Yatsuki frequents. Her maid is "Moru." Prone by nature to being possessed by spirits and yokai.

AYATSUKI ROKKA
A pretty girl whom Yatsuki once helped out. She seems quite taken with him since then. She's actually a yokai: a rokurokubi.

NISHIZURU YATSUKI
Works part-time in Akihabara. Can see ghosts and has gotten himself mixed up with a bunch of yokai.

NISHIZURU NANAO
Yatsuki's sister. She's been stuck as a spirit for the past six years, unable to return to her comatose body.

KAPPER-VERT-SAN!!

YOU'RE GETTING CARRIED AWAY!

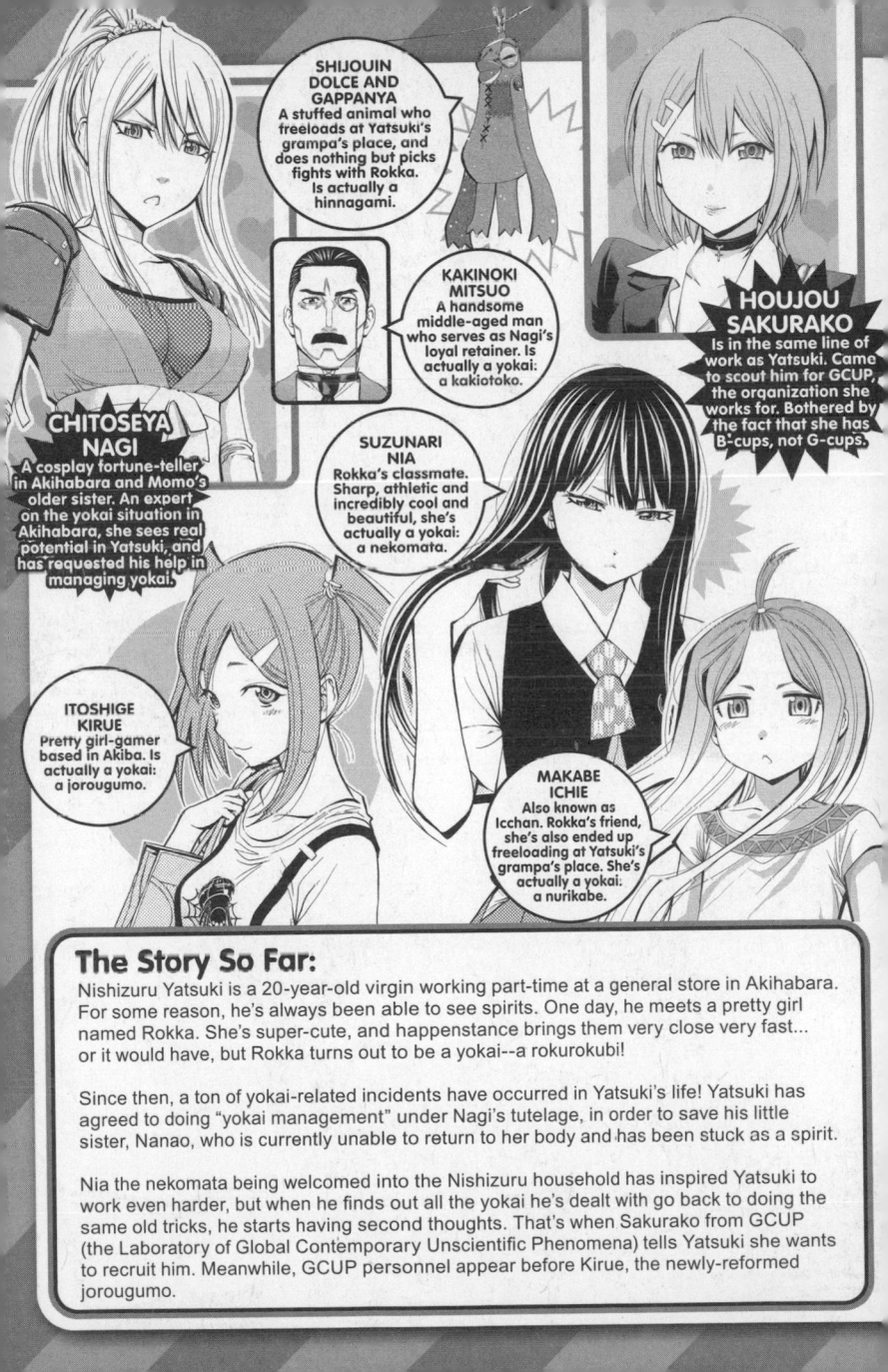

SHIJOUIN DOLCE AND GAPPANYA
A stuffed animal who freeloads at Yatsuki's grampa's place, and does nothing but picks fights with Rokka. Is actually a hinnagami.

KAKINOKI MITSUO
A handsome middle-aged man who serves as Nagi's loyal retainer. Is actually a yokai: a kakiotoko.

HOUJOU SAKURAKO
Is in the same line of work as Yatsuki. Came to scout him for GCUP, the organization she works for. Bothered by the fact that she has B-cups, not G-cups.

CHITOSEYA NAGI
A cosplay fortune-teller in Akihabara and Momo's older sister. An expert on the yokai situation in Akihabara, she sees real potential in Yatsuki, and has requested his help in managing yokai.

SUZUNARI NIA
Rokka's classmate. Sharp, athletic and incredibly cool and beautiful, she's actually a yokai: a nekomata.

ITOSHIGE KIRUE
Pretty girl-gamer based in Akiba. Is actually a yokai: a jorougumo.

MAKABE ICHIE
Also known as Icchan. Rokka's friend, she's also ended up freeloading at Yatsuki's grampa's place. She's actually a yokai: a nurikabe.

The Story So Far:

Nishizuru Yatsuki is a 20-year-old virgin working part-time at a general store in Akihabara. For some reason, he's always been able to see spirits. One day, he meets a pretty girl named Rokka. She's super-cute, and happenstance brings them very close very fast... or it would have, but Rokka turns out to be a yokai--a rokurokubi!

Since then, a ton of yokai-related incidents have occurred in Yatsuki's life! Yatsuki has agreed to doing "yokai management" under Nagi's tutelage, in order to save his little sister, Nanao, who is currently unable to return to her body and has been stuck as a spirit.

Nia the nekomata being welcomed into the Nishizuru household has inspired Yatsuki to work even harder, but when he finds out all the yokai he's dealt with go back to doing the same old tricks, he starts having second thoughts. That's when Sakurako from GCUP (the Laboratory of Global Contemporary Unscientific Phenomena) tells Yatsuki she wants to recruit him. Meanwhile, GCUP personnel appear before Kirue, the newly-reformed jorougumo.

YOKAI GIRLS

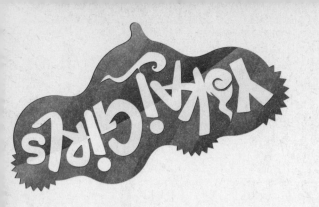

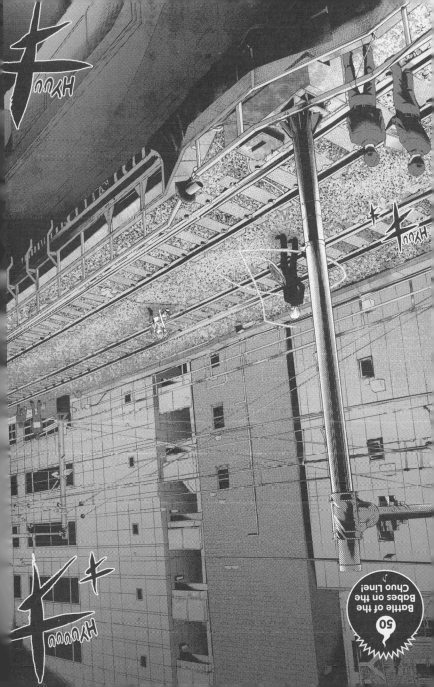

Battle of the Babes on the Chuo Line!

HUNH
YOU MAY BE GCUP, BUT YOU'RE DIFFERENT FROM THE SMALL FRY I'VE SHAKEN OFF BEFORE
GUESS IT'S TIME FOR THE MID-GAME BOSS, HUH?
FOR YOU...
I'M THE FINAL BOSS.
AND THE ENDING...
ZAA
HYUUN
IS A HAPPY ONE... THAT ENDS WITH YOUR DEATH!

......
TOUCH
THE WOUND ISN'T CLOSING UP.
HIS WEAPON... THAT WASN'T JUST A PHYSICAL ATTACK?!
ME, DEAD?
HA!
YOU THINK I CAN'T ESCAPE A BASIC ENCIR-CLEMENT LIKE THIS?
YOU WON'T GET AWAY.
SNAP
RATTLE KATAN
TZING
TZING
TZING
TA-TUNK TUNK

BZZT...
?!
BZZT
AN LTP NET.
WE'VE COATED ULTRA-HARD, RAZOR-SHARPENED WIRE WITH LTP.
EVEN A YOKAI WON'T GO UNSCATHED IF THEY TOUCH IT.

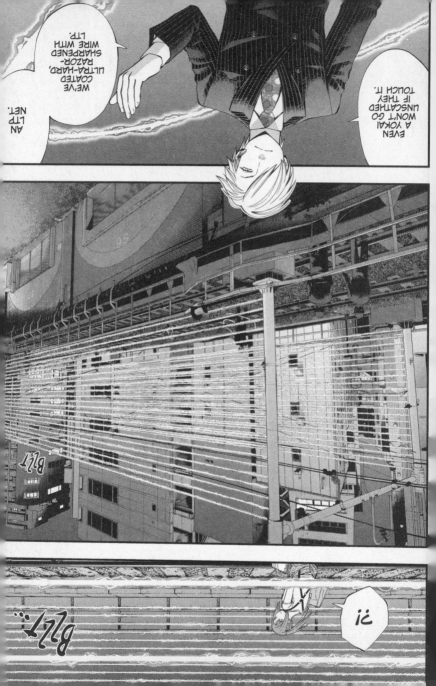

EL TEEPEE?
I DON'T GET WHAT THAT IS, BUT IT SEEMS TO CAUSE THE SAME DAMAGE AS HIS WEAPON.
SO, IT'S SOMETHING ELSE THAT CAN DAMAGE US, HUH?
BZZT
MY ESCAPE IS CUT OFF ON EITHER SIDE.
SO, ABOVE ...?
DRIP
TCH!
DRIP

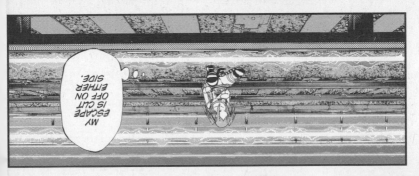

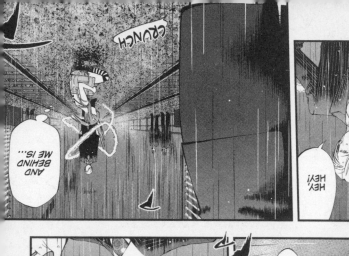

CRUNCH

...AND BEHIND ME IS...

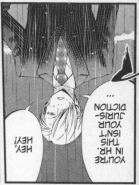

...

YOU'RE IN HR. THIS ISN'T YOUR JURIS-DICTION

HEY, HEY!

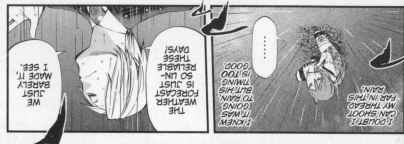

WE JUST BARELY MADE IT, I SEE.

THE WEATHER FORECAST IS JUST SO UN-RELIABLE THESE DAYS!

......

I KNEW IT WAS GOING TO RAIN, BUT THIS TIMING IS TOO GOOD.

I DOUBT I CAN SHOOT MY THREAD FAR IN THIS RAIN.

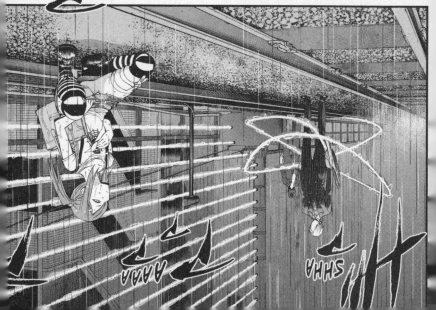

AAAA

SHHA

SAKU-RAKO-SAN!
AW~! ♪ 'CMON!
LET ME HAVE A LITTLE FUN, TOO! ♡
......
WELL, YOU...
SHAAA
CAN TRY!
ZAA

WHOOPS!
SLIDE-UN
!
HYU HYUU
TCH!!
TWUF
TWUF
SLICE
GACHA
VITA
STAY OUT OF THIS, YUKIMURA-KUN!
DASH
!!
HYUU
ZAA

GA-KLANG
BWOO
DO
DO-DON
DON
DO DO DO
HEH
...

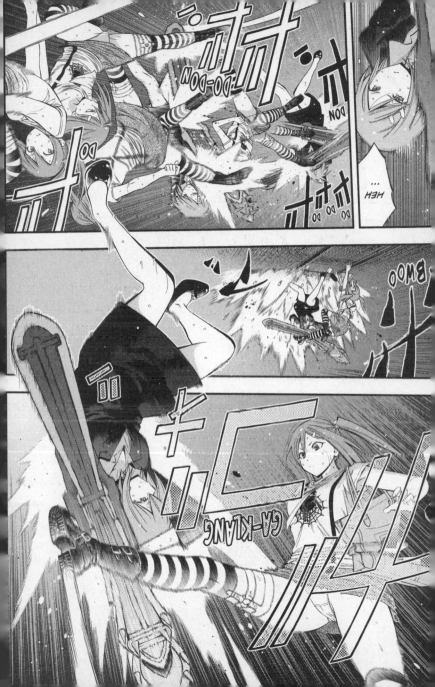

GA-CHING
FWIP
AH!
NIP SLIP—!
ZU ZA ZA
TUMP
SHE'S...
HYUHYUN
HYUN

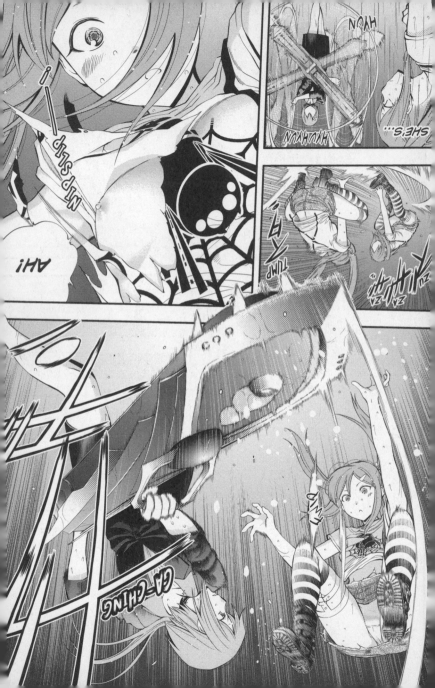

GA-CHING
NO ORDINARY WOMAN!!
NOT BAD AT ALL!
SHA
I ACTUALLY USED TO BE A B-LEVEL HOUND, YOU KNOW.
THANK YOU! ♡
AA
BUT...
A
YOU'RE SLOW!!

!
GYUUN
OH NO!
HER THREAD!
CLOP
SHE STOPPED?!
BO BO
OKAY...
TAKE THIS!

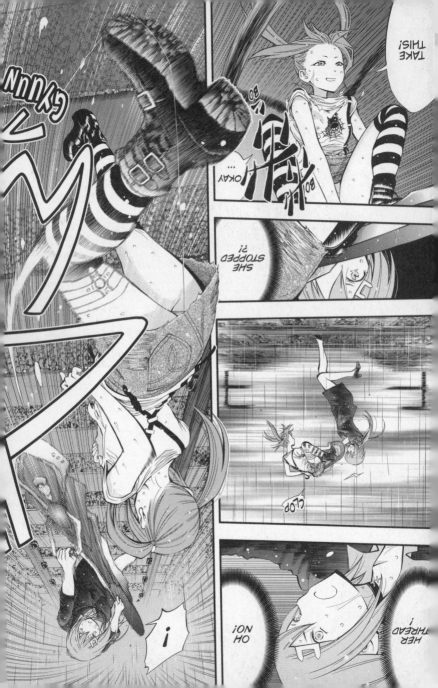

HEYYY ?!
BOOTY SHOT!
AT LEAST I LEFT YOU SOME DIGNITY. ♡
Ooh! ♡
A sheer G-string! ♡
GA-SHAA
How risqué.
My, my.
YOU...
BLUSH
BITCH!

GA-KLANG
SORRRY~!
FSHT
YOU WILL BE!
KISS OF CAPTIVA-TION!!
BWOO

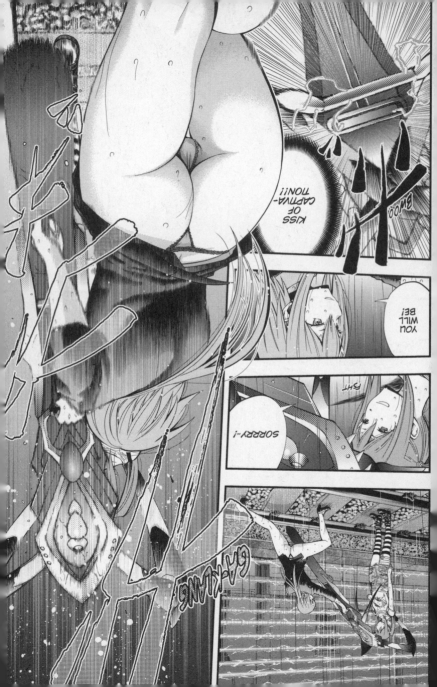

SPLUK
AGH ...
SLASH
AH...
STAGGER

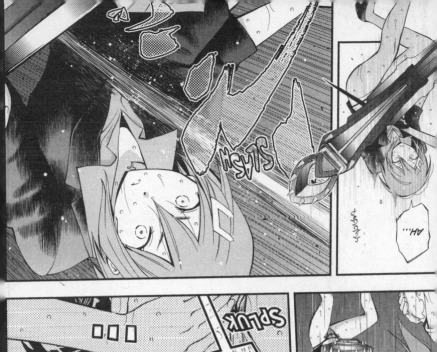

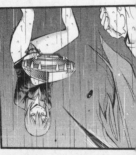

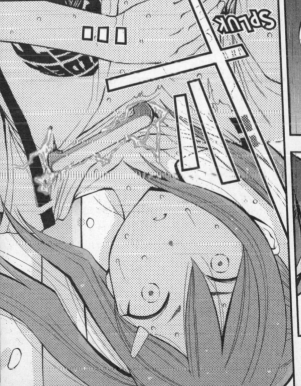

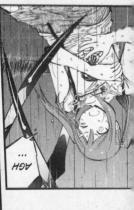

ZA ZA...
NGH...
......
THAT WAS CLOSE.
IF I HADN'T BEEN WEARING MY BEAR SUIT, I'D BE OUT!
NGH ...
AHH !!
YANK
HAAH...
THIS IS... THE SAME KIND OF WEAPON.
WHAT THE HELL ...
ARE THESE GUYS ?!
CLANG
HAAH...
DRIP DRIP
......

SHA
HEH!
I SEE!
!
SHA
JUST WHAT YOU'D EXPECT FROM A C-CLASS NE.
SHA
YOU'RE A DIFFICULT ONE TO MANAGE!
I'VE HAD ENOUGH.
SHA
I'D RATHER NOT BE EMBARRASSED ANY FURTHER IN FRONT OF MY COLLEAGUE.
I'LL STEP ASIDE FOR OUR STAR PERFORMER!
SHA
Yes.
Please do.
SHA
SHA
YOU HANDLE THE REST...
HUH ...?

SHAAA
NISHIZURU YATSUKI-KUN!
SHA
SHAA

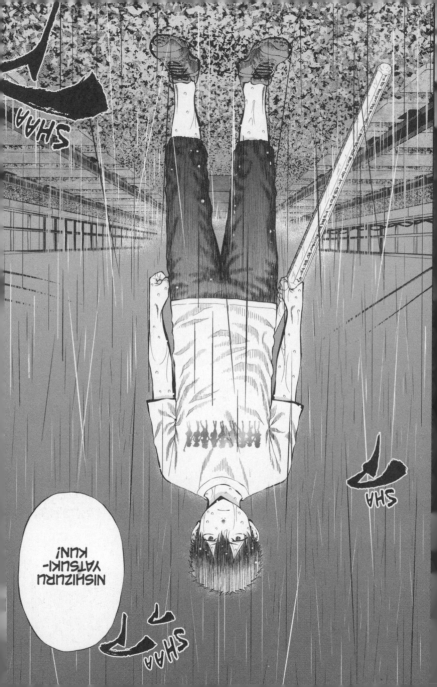

YOU HANDLE THE REST...
SHAA
GRUNCH
SHAA
NISHIZURU YATSUKI-KUN!
SHAA
51 Doesn't Stink Any-more!♪
H-HUH?!
H-HOUJOU-SAN?! YOUR CLOTHES ...
YOUR WHOLE BUTT IS HANGING OUT!!
YEEEEK!
DON'T LOOK !!
HEY, LEND ME A JACK-ET!
R-RIGHT!
SHA
!
SHA
HUH?

51 Doesn't Stink Any-more! ♪

SHA
HIME...
SHAAAA
CHAN?
SHA

YATSUKI ...
SHA

A PROPOSAL?
COFFEE & TEA PLACE
COFFEE SALON PLACE
YES!
WE'VE GOT AN OPERATION TONIGHT TO SUBDUE A MAJOR NE!
WE'D LIKE YOU TO HELP US OUT!
UM, "NE"?
WEL-COME!
SO!
TP
"NE" AS IN NON-EXISTENT.
YEAH, IT REFERS TO YOKAI.
THAT'S WHAT WE CALL YOKAI!
SOME-THING THAT DOESN'T EXIST... SO...IN ORDER TO EXIST...
!
YOU'RE FINALLY HERE.
ABOUT TIME...

YUKI-MURA-KUN!
OH?
JUST NOW, THERE WAS THIS WOMAN OUTSIDE GLARING AT YOU WITH THE MOST INTENSE LOOK ON HER FACE.
HUH?! WHO?!
I DON'T KNOW!
YOU'RE ALWAYS TICKING GIRLS OFF, AREN'T YOU?
SHUT UP!!
People will get the wrong idea!
WHOOPS! COULD YOU STAY BACK, PLEASE?
MY PER-SONAL SPACE IS ONE METER.
STOP!
ENOUGH OF THAT! JUST GET OVER HERE!
LET ME INTRODUCE YOU TO YUKIMURA JUNSEI-KUN!
Hmm!
HE LOOKS ABOUT 167CM TALL... I SUPPOSE HIS SITTING HEIGHT IS ABOUT 90CM...
He's got short legs.
HE'S ANTI-NE COMBAT PERSONNEL, THE PRIDE OF GCUP!
COM-BAT...
HE'S ONE OF WHAT WE CALL "THE HOUNDS."
HOUNDS...

I'D LOVE IT IF YOU COULD WORK WITH HIM ON TONIGHT'S OPERATION!
IF YOU DO, I THINK WE CAN HELP YOU WITH YOUR SISTER.
YOU'LL BE A COL-LABORATOR. AS SUCH, WE CAN GIVE YOU SOME INFORMATION.
I'D FEEL BETTER GOING ALONE, THOUGH.
QUIET, YOU!
TOGETH-ER...
......
UH...
OKAY!
I DON'T KNOW IF I CAN BE USEFUL TO YOU, BUT IF YOU'RE OKAY WITH ME HELPING...
THANKS! WE'LL BE COUNTING ON YOU.

HI! SHA?

NISHIZURU YATSUKI-KUN!

SHA

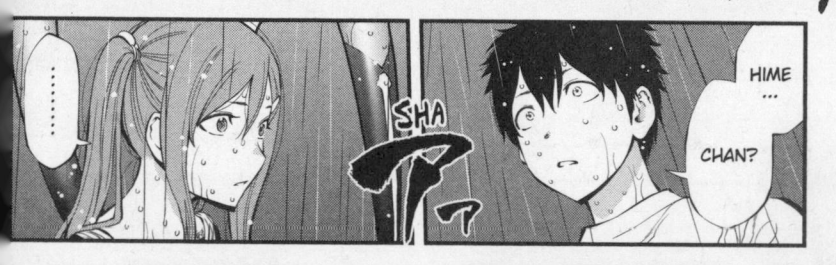

・・・・・・・・・

SHA?

HIME...

CHAN?

THIS IS THE JOROU-GUMO YOU LET ESCAPE.

THAT'S RIGHT.

HOUJOU-SAN! THIS IS...!

HEY...

HOW DO YOU KNOW ABOUT THAT?!

!

SHA

SHAA

YOU DESTROYED HER BARRIER, DIDN'T YOU?
SHA
THANKS TO YOU, A NUMBER OF BODIES RETURNED TO THE REAL WORLD.
IN OTHER WORDS, YOU BROUGHT THEM TO THE LIGHT.
SHA
ALONG WITH THE FACT OF HER EXISTENCE!
SHA
THAT TIME...
THE DESTRUCTION OF A C-CLASS NE BARRIER IS VERY UNCOMMON!
WE WONDERED IF THIS WAS AN EXCEPTIONAL PSYCHIC, OR A FALLING-OUT BETWEEN NES.
IF IT WERE THE FORMER, THEY COULD BE A POWERFUL ASSET!
SHA
GCUP LOOKED FOR THE CAUSE, HOPING IT WOULD BE THE FORMER.
AND WHAT WE FOUND...
SHA

WAS YOU...
SHA
NISHIZURU YATSUKI-KUN!
COME ON!
THIS TIME, LET'S MAKE SURE TO BURY IT FOR GOOD--TOGETHER!
SHA
I CAN'T...
SHA
I SEE.
SAYING THANK YOU, OR ASKING ME TO PLAY GUILTY GEAR...
SHA
!
YOU JUST WANTED ME TO LET MY GUARD DOWN.
ALL FOR THIS.
NO!
THAT'S NOT IT, HIME-CHAN! THERE'S A REASON--
ENOUGH ALREADY!
SHA
I GET IT NOW.
CLENCH

SHAA
I WAS AN IDIOT FOR TRUSTING A HUMAN!
SHAA
GWOO

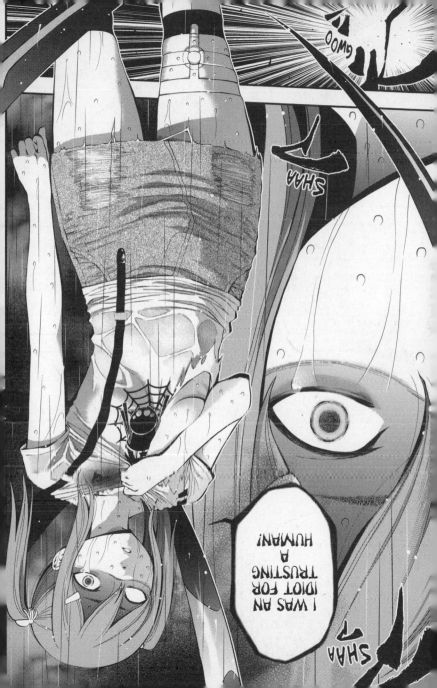

BA-THWACK
KRIK KRIK
NGH...
KRIK KRIK
TP
AGH...
DAN
GA-SHING
BA
BA

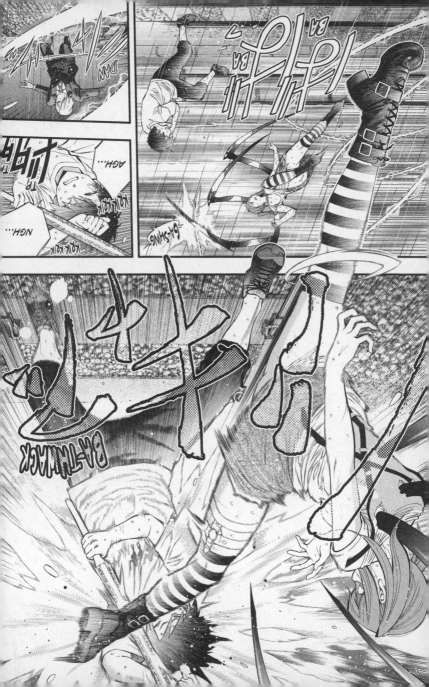

GAN
GAN
GAN
ZU-GAN
YOU'VE GOT IT ALL WRONG!
NGH!
GA-GAN
DON
GAN
GAN
IT'S NOT WHAT YOU THINK, HIME-CHAN!
GA-GAN
AMAZING! HER ATTACKS ARE SO INTENSE, BUT HE'S DEFLECTING ALL OF THEM!
GA-GAN
AND WITH A MERE WOODEN SWORD!
GA-
GAN
GAN
HOUJOU-SAN! SHE'S NOT LIKE THAT!!
HIME-CHAN'S NOT ATTACKING PEOPLE ANYMORE!
HUH?
GAN
GAN

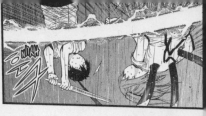

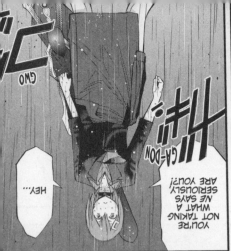

HEY....

YOU'RE NOT TAKING ME SAYS WHAT A SERIOUSLY ARE YOU?!

GIVE ME A BREAK!

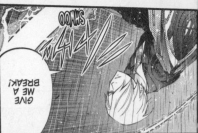

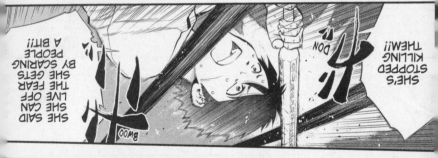

SHE SAID SHE CAN LIVE OFF THE FEAR SHE GETS BY SCARING PEOPLE A BIT!!

SHE'S STOPPED KILLING THEM!!

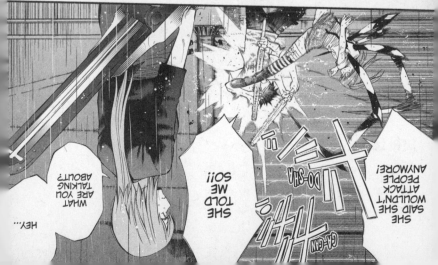

HEY....

WHAT ARE YOU TALKING ABOUT?

SHE TOLD ME SO!!

SHE SAID SHE WOULDN'T ATTACK PEOPLE ANYMORE!

YOU STAY OUT OF THIS!!
GA-KLAAANG
!!
HE KICKED IT...
WITH HIS FOOT?!
IT'S NOT ABOUT TRUST OR WHAT-EVER!

HIME-CHAN...
DOESN'T STINK ANYMORE!!

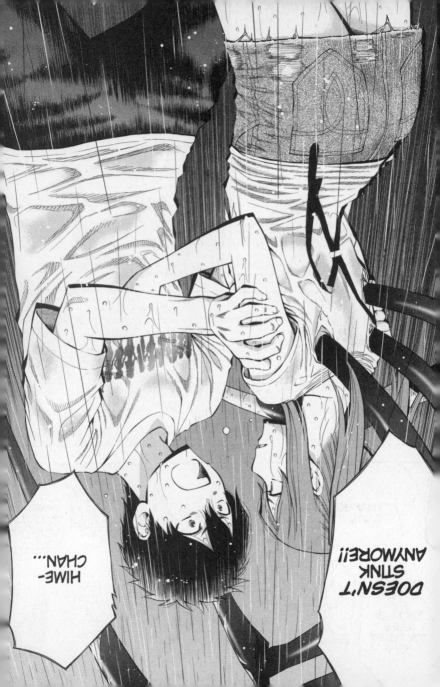

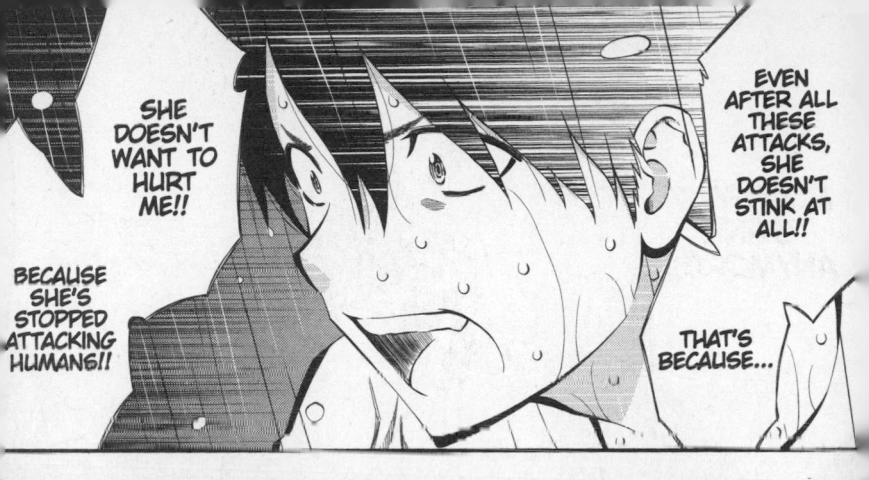

SHE DOESN'T WANT TO HURT ME!!

EVEN AFTER ALL THESE ATTACKS, SHE DOESN'T STINK AT ALL!!

BECAUSE SHE'S STOPPED ATTACKING HUMANS!!

THAT'S BECAUSE...

YATSUKI...

RIGHT, HIME-CHAN?!

SHE'S NOT OUR ENEMY ANY-MORE!!

POS-SESSED BY THAT JOROU-GUMO!

IT SEEMS HE'S BEEN...

THAT COULDN'T BE.

NO WAY...

FWOo...

HYUN HYUU

HE'S NO USE.

GOOD GRIEF!

G-SPIN
BASH!!
SCREE SCREE
I TOLD YOU TO STAY OUT OF THIS!!
YATSUKI...
Your hand!
UNFORTUNATELY...
IT SEEMS YOU'RE RIGHT.
!!
CRUNCH

KISS OF CAPTIVA-TION!!
BAN
AH...
GEH...
HIME-CHA--

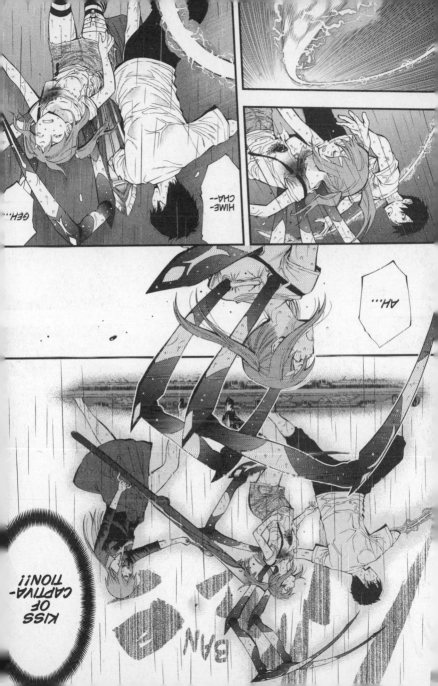

DON!!
SHLK

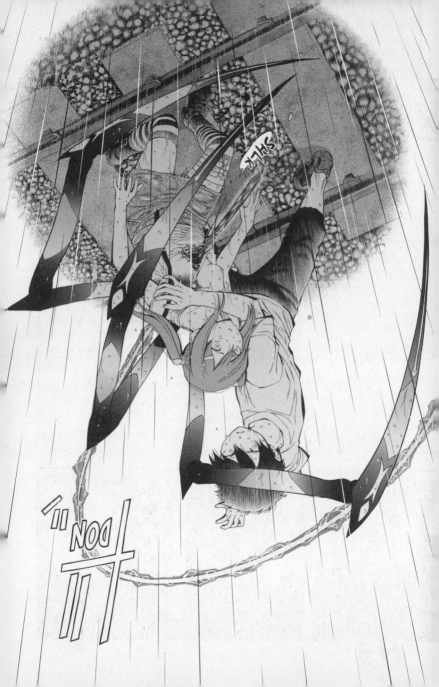

52
As a Human... ♪
SHA
HNGGH!
A hook-and-ladder truck?
A
WHAT THE HECK IS JUNKER-SAN DOING...
SNEAKING OUT SO LATE AT NIGHT?!
DID HE GET A CON-STRUCTION JOB OR SOME-THING?
GLANCE
GLANCE
No one's around.
Yep?
SHURURU
Hup!
Let's take a peek!
AA
BZZT...

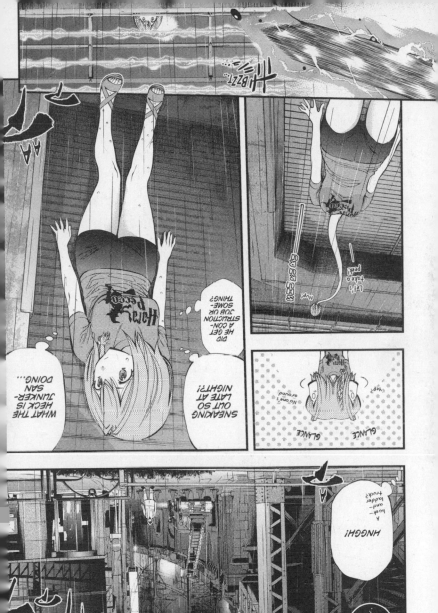

52
As a Human... ♪
STAGGER

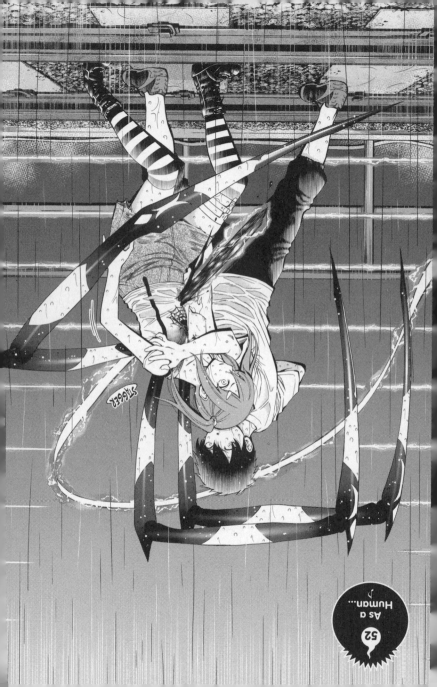

KAH...
HGH...
SPLURT
HIME...
SHUPA
STO--
SWING
UGH...
STOOOOOP!!!

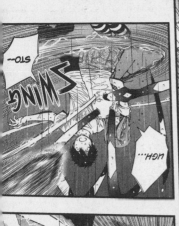

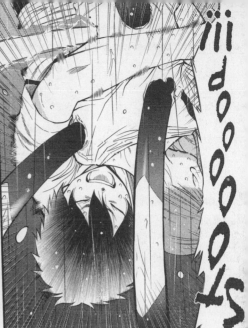

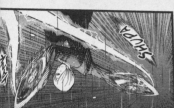

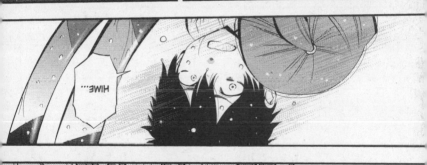

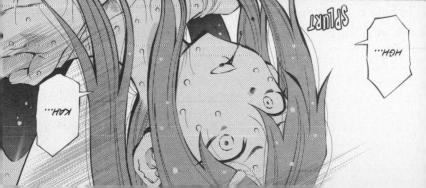

AH...
AHHH...
HBZZZP

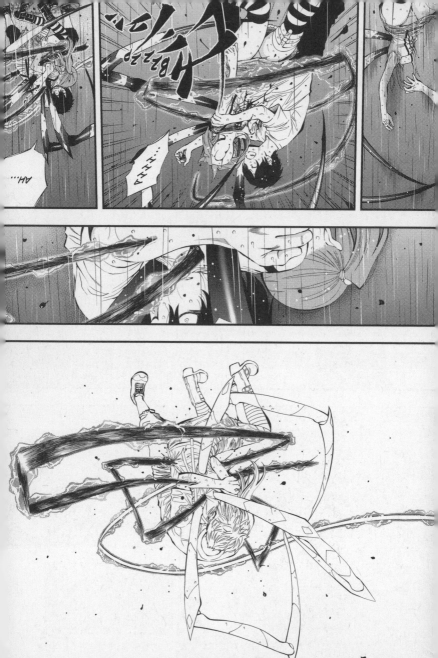

SHA
AH...
SHA
!!
HOUJOU-SAN! THE DETECTOR IS REACTING TO A NEW NE!
!
SHA
CLASS AND DISTANCE ?!
TWELVE METERS STRAIGHT DOWN! IT'S RIGHT UNDER US!
E!
SHA
SHA
SHA
HN, IT DISAP-PEARED.
......
SO IT RAN AWAY.
......
SHA

IT'S HER.
DIGESTIVE FLUIDS INTO THIS GIRL, INSTEAD.
EEP...!
THIS IS MY NEST! IT GOES ON FOREVER
YOU CAN'T RUN FROM ME!
A SPIDER !!
LOTS OF GAMERS GO.
HMPH
SO. JUNKER-SAN INVITES ALL THE GIRLS OUT TO CURRY...?
A SPIDER YOKAI!!!
SHA
AH...
AHH!
SHA
YOU CAN'T...
SHA
IT'LL BE OKAY!
WEAPONS CAN'T...
YOU CAN'T, HIME-CHAN!
SHA
I MEAN, PHYSICAL ATTACKS CAN'T KILL YOKAI, RIGHT?!
SHA
YOU CAN'T DIE!
IT'LL BE OKAY! IT'LL BE OKAY!
YATSU ...
KI...

SHA
CRYING... FOR ME?
BUT...
I'M A YOKAI...
SHA
SHA
WH...
WHAT'S THAT GOT TO DO WITH ANY-THING?!
I PROMISED YOU, DIDN'T I?! THAT WE'D GO ON A DATE!!
WE'RE GONNA PLAY GUILTY GEAR, RIGHT?!
SHA
SHA
I'LL...
PRACTICE, OKAY?!
I'LL GET GOOD ENOUGH THAT YOU WON'T BEAT ME... I SWEAR!
SHA
SHA
HA!
GASP
THERE'S... NO WAY...
GASP
YOU'RE ...
SUCH A NOOB...
SO...
YATSU ...
YOU... KNOW...
SOB ...
KI...

I WISH... I COULD HAVE...
MET YOU... EARLIER...

IF I CAN...
SOB...
AH...
BE REBORN AGAIN... NEXT TIME...

I HOPE I'M A HUMAN.
TUMP

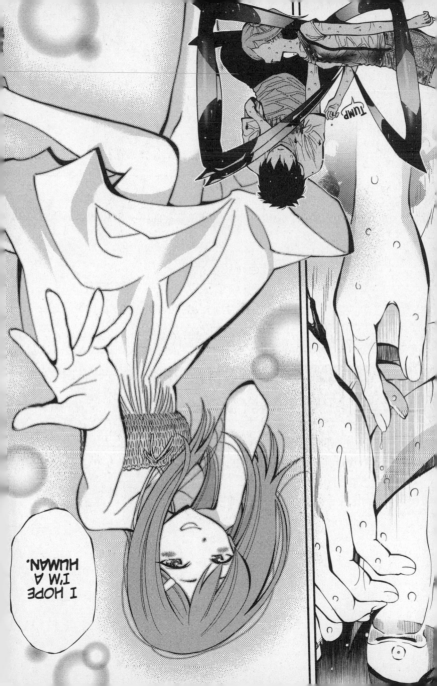

HIME...
SHAA
CHAN?
SHAAAA
NO.
SHA
NO...
YOU CAN'T DIE.
YOU CAN'T DIE, YOU CAN'T DIE!
SHA
HNGH...
SHA
YOU CAN'T ...
SOB...
SHAA

わぁぁあぁあぁあ
WAAAAAAGH!
THE JOROUGUMO'S NE REACTION HAS DISAPPEARED!
AAAAAAGH...
IF HE'S REALLY POSSESSED, THEN HE SHOULD REGAIN HIS SENSES ONCE THE NE THAT POSSESSED HIM IS DEAD.
WHAT DOES THIS MEAN?
IT COULDN'T BE...
HE SERIOUSLY ...?
AGHAHA...
HA HA!
CRUNCH
ITS LEGS CURLED IN WHEN IT DIED, JUST LIKE A SPIDER!

SHAAAAA
MOVE IT!
I'M GOING TO SLICE IT UP TO MAKE ABSOLUTELY SURE IT CAN'T REVIVE!
YOU ...
BASTARD ...
MOVE IT!
GASHI
!!

C'MON! WHAT DO YOU THINK YOU'RE DOING?
SHAAAA
HIME-CHAN...
SHA
HIME-CHAN...
DIDN'T STINK ANY-MORE!
SHE'D REFORMED. SHE'D HAD A CHANGE OF HEART!
HEY...
BUT YOU BASTARDS...
SHA
YOU'LL LOSE YOUR FINGERS IF YOU DON'T LET GO!
AND YOU...
I'LL NEVER FORGIVE YOU FOR THIS!!!
SHAA
GRIND

SHLK
?!
WHA ...?
WHY ...?!
GAH ...
AH...
YANK
GEH...
COME...
BA-THUMP
BA-THUMP
A-THUMP
COME ...!!

COME ON, ROKKA !!!
BA-THUMP
HE'S CALLING ME...
FUWA...
ふわ…
JUNKER-SAN IS...

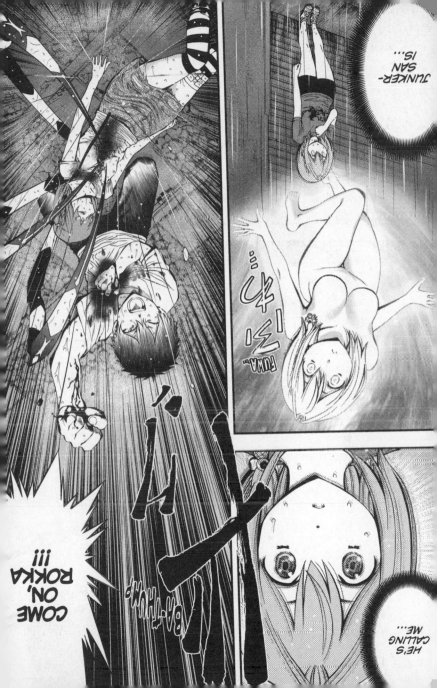

CALLING ME!!
H-HOUJOU-SAN! THERE'S AN NE REACTION!
WHA...?
WHAT IS HAPPENING?!
NISHIZURU-SAN'S ETHEREAL ENERGY LEVELS ARE INCREASING DRAMATICALLY!
THIS IS...
WHOA!
KIIII
YEEK!

ETHEREAL
FUSION!!!
AAGH...
INSTANT FIRE!!!

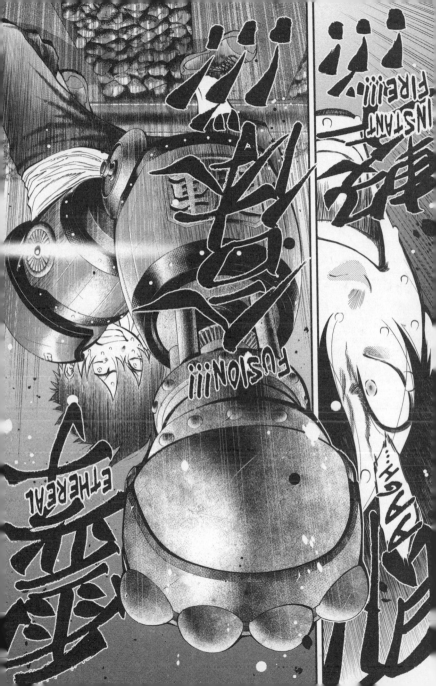

ZU-DON
HEADBUTT
BLITZ!!!!!

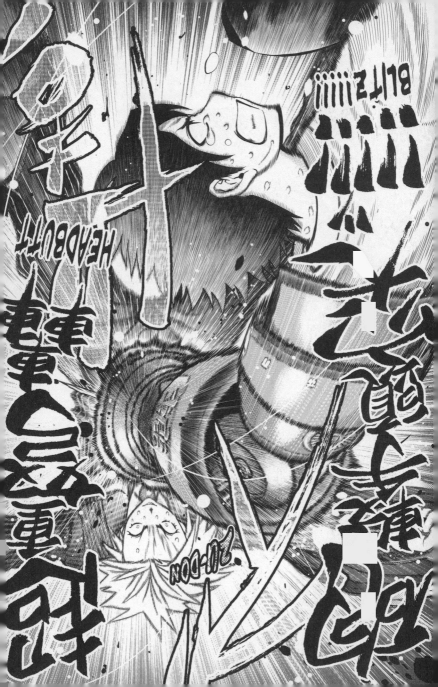

WAUGH...
即撃ッ!!!
INSTANT FIRE!!!
超重警轟砲撃頭突ッ!!!!!!
HEADBUTT BLITZ!!!!!
AAGH...
ZU-DON

THUD
DA
DA
DA
DON
PATTER
HYUN HYUN
PATTER
GAN
PATTER
SHAA
GACHINK
NO WAY... YUKIMURA-SAN IS AN A-RANK HOUND. AND HE WENT DOWN IN ONE HIT!
H-HOUJOU-SAN! NISHIZURU-SAN'S ETHEREAL POWER LEVELS ARE ESCALATING RAPIDLY!
NISHIZURU-KUN... JUST WHAT...
THIS IS A-CLASS... NO. THIS IS...

53
Distance: Zero! ♪
SHA
S-CLASS LEVEL!!
PANT ...
PANT ...
SHAA
PANT ...
SHAAA
JUST WHAT ON EARTH ARE YOU?!!

SHAAA
LTP STANDS FOR...
SHA
"LOW TEMPERATURE PLASMA."
IT'S AN ABBRE-VIATION OF THE ENGLISH TERM.
LOW-TEMPER-ATURE PLASMA?
THAT'S RIGHT.
FIRST, LET'S BEGIN WITH AN EXPLANATION OF PLASMA.

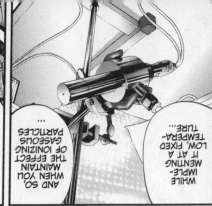

...

AND SO, WHEN YOU MAINTAIN THE EFFECT OF IONIZING GASEOUS PARTICLES

WHILE IMPLE-MENTING IT AT A LOW, FIXED TEMPERA-TURE....

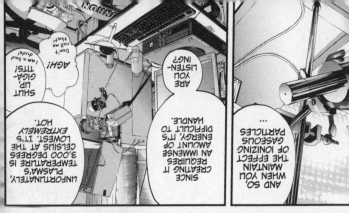

SHUT UP GIGA-ITS!

AGH!

I am a bad dude! Don't call me that!

ARE YOU LISTEN-ING?

UNFORTUNATELY, PLASMA'S TEMPERATURE IS 3,000 DEGREES CELSIUS AT THE LOWEST. IT'S EXTREMELY HOT.

SINCE CREATING IT REQUIRES AN IMMENSE AMOUNT OF ENERGY, IT'S DIFFICULT TO HANDLE.

MOCO-CHAN! CAN'T A GIRL CALL HERSELF A 'BAD DUDE'!

WHAT'RE YOU TAKING ABOUT?

PUT IT IN TERMS A BAD DUDE LIKE ME CAN UNDER-STAND.

IF YOU USE THIS EFFECT, THERE ARE VARIOUS THINGS YOU CAN DO WITH IT: HIGH-SPEED RELEASE OF SEMICONDUCTOR RESISTANCE, OR DISPOSAL OF POISONOUS GASES THROUGH DISINTEGRATION....

AND WHEN PLASMA COMES IN CONTACT WITH OTHER MATTER, IT REACTS WITH IT, AND HAS THE EFFECT OF TURNING THAT OTHER MATTER INTO PLASMA AS WELL.

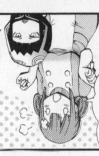

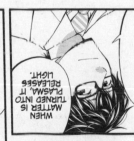

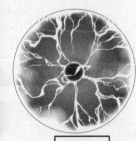

LIKE, PLASMA TVS AND STUFF?

THE SUN, LIGHTNING, AND THE NORTHERN LIGHTS ARE A KIND OF PLASMA, RIGHT?

A PLASMA TV IS A DEVICE THAT USES THAT LIGHT!

WHEN MATTER IS TURNED INTO PLASMA, IT RELEASES LIGHT.

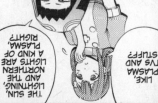

IT'S A STATE WHERE THE MOLECULES THAT COMPRISE A GAS PARTIALLY OR COMPLETELY IONIZE.

PLASMA IS A FOURTH STATE OF MATTER THAT FOLLOWS SOLID, LIQUID AND GAS.

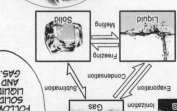

Solid — Melting → Liquid
Liquid — Freezing → Solid
Evaporation / Condensation
Sublimation
Gas — Ionization → Plasma
Plasma — Recombination → Gas

YOU GET LOW-TEMPER-ATURE PLASMA!
LTP!
......
STILL TOO MUCH, HUH?
ALL RIGHT! I'LL SHOW YOU!
DO YOU KNOW WHAT THIS IS?
IS IT... IRON?
NAH, IT'S RUSTY COPPER.
WHEN YOU TOUCH LTP TO THIS...

BECAUSE IT DISSOCIATED THE OXYGEN (O) ATOMS FROM THE COPPER OXIDE (CuO)!
THE RUST ...!
SO THIS IS HOW YOU CAN DESTROY THE MOLECULAR GEOMETRY OF AN NE USING LTP!
NE ALL HAVE POWERFUL ETHEREAL BODIES.
NO MATTER HOW MUCH YOU INJURE THEIR PHYSICAL BODIES, THEY WILL INSTANTLY REGENERATE WITH ENERGY FROM THEIR ETHEREAL BODIES.
IN ORDER TO WOUND THEM FATALLY, YOU NEED TO DAMAGE THEIR ETHEREAL BODIES, TOO.
AND THE ETHEREAL BODY...
IS JUST MATTER COMPOSED OF ETHER!

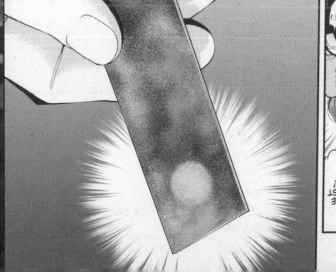

AS LONG AS IT'S COMPOSED OF MATTER...
LTP CAN DESTROY IT EASILY!
SHAAAA
SHA
SHAA
HIME-CHAN ...
SHA
JUNKER-SAN...

YOU PUNCHED ME.
YOU DIDN'T JUST VIOLATE MY PERSONAL SPACE...
YOU...
YOU TOUCHED MY BODY.
GWO
GWO
DIS-TANCE...
ZERO.
ZERO.
ZERO.
THAT ISN'T AL-LOWED!
ZERO...
ZERO...
SHLUNK
GWO
ZERO ZERO ZERO ZERO ZERO ZERO...!
GWO
WITH MY IRON RULE OF JUDG-MENT...
ZERO...

ZERO!
I WILL MEASURE ...
ZERO ...
ZERO ...
YOUR SINS!!

HE'S UP?!
I DIDN'T CHARGE UP, BUT THAT WAS STILL A POINT-BLANK HIT!

HEY ...
THIS IS BAD! HE'S LOST IT!
WHEN YUKI-MURA-KUN GETS LIKE THAT, HE...
HOLD ON, UKIMURA-KU--!

1026!
BYUU
WHOA ...
GRSSH
HYUUN
HYUUN
HYUU
ROKKA ?!
I'M OKAY, YEP!
SO, WHEN ROKKA'S LIKE THIS, SHE CAN BLOCK THAT WEAPON'S ATTACKS!
HYUU
DASH DASH DASH
SCREEE
THEN...
HYUUN

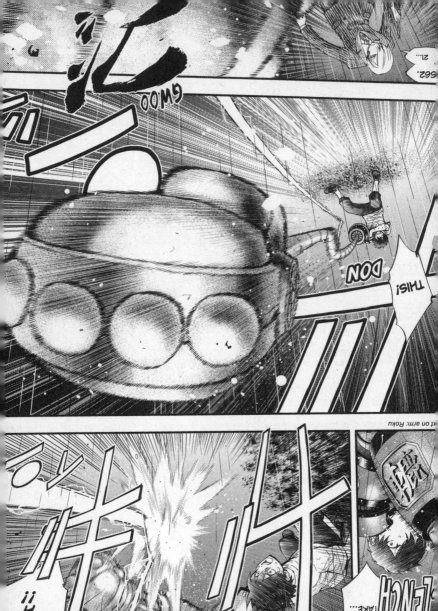

GWOO

DON

THIS!

t on arm: Roku

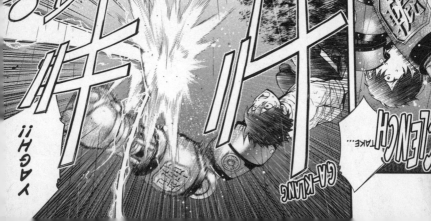

GA-KLANG

2LENGH TAKE...

YAGH!!

18...!
BWOO
623...
ZAZA
412...
112.5!
OOF...
GA-SHING
WHOOPS, WRONG WAY.
131.
GA-CHING
HE DODG-ED IT?!
NGH ...!

DON
KYUN
7...!
245...
426...
BA
BA
BA
BA
CRAP!
DON
DON
JUNKER-SAN!
SHOOTING RANDOMLY ISN'T GONNA...
HE KEEPS JUMPING AROUND!
24!
BWOO
46!
ZAZA

DASH
482!
DASH
DASH
ZA
......
DASH
DASH
453!
RGH...
GURUU
389!
TOO SLOW!
GAH!
PSHOO

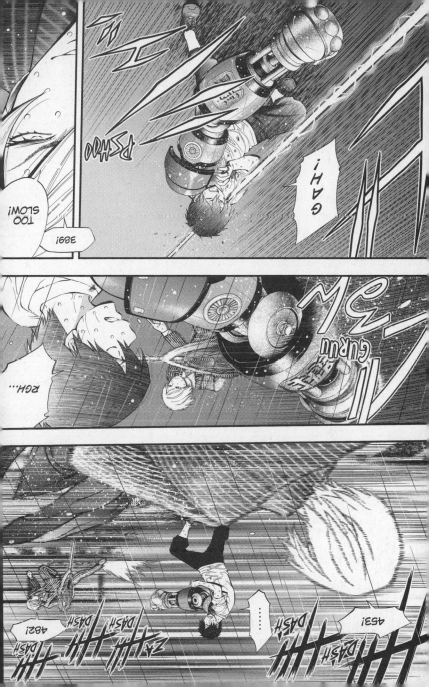

HA!
BA
THAT ARM PACKS A PUNCH, BUT ITS TRAJECTORY IS DIRECT AND DULL!!
BA
BA
IT RETURNS SLOWLY AFTER FIRING, AND YOU CAN'T FIRE CONTINUOUS SHOTS!
BYUU
BA
BA
BA
IT'S EASY TO DODGE AFTER SEEING IT ONCE!
NGH...
BA
DAMN IT! WHAT THE HELL IS WITH THAT WEAPON OF HIS?!
WHOA...
BA
BA
BA-CHING
IT HURTS LIKE HELL! LIKE IT'S CUTTING INTO MY SOUL!
BA
AND IT CAN BEND AND TRANSFORM, TOO. I CAN NEVER PREDICT WHERE HE'S GOING TO HIT!
BA
BA
SHIING
JUNKER-SAN! YOU CAN'T JUST GO ON A SOLO RAMPAGE!
WE HAVE TO WORK AS A TEAM!!
HA! WHAT'S WRONG? YOU FANATIC, COMPLICIT WITH THE NE, ENEMY OF HUMANITY!
BA
IS THAT ALL YOU'VE GOT?!
WHAT SHOULD I DO?!
CLANG
NE? THE ENEMY OF HUMANITY?!
NGH...
BA
HYUU
HIME-CHAN DIDN'T SMELL ANYMORE! AND YOU--
BA

I CAN TELL BY SCENT!!
YOKAI AND SPIRITS WITH EVIL INTENT ALWAYS STINK!
BUT HIME-CHAN DIDN'T SMELL ANY-MORE!!
YOU'VE BEEN GOING ON AND ON ABOUT STINKING AND NOT STINKING! WHAT ARE YOU TALKING ABOUT?!
AND THAT!
HE'S STOPPED ATTACK-ING?!
Haah!
I SEE.
Haah!
JUNKER-SAN!!
THEN LET ME ASK YOU THIS...
PSYCHIC.
HYUUHYUN
?!

EVIL INTENT..
TOWARDS WHOM?

?!

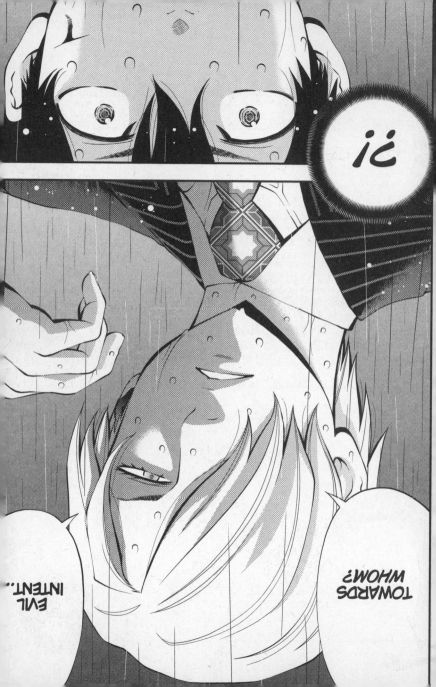

SHAA
EVIL INTENT...
54
The Reality of Evil Intent... ♪
SHA
TOWARDS WHOM?
SHAAAA
SHA
HUH?

TOWARDS YOU, PERSON-ALLY?
TOWARDS HUMANITY? TOWARDS ALL LIVING THINGS?
SHAAAA
OR IS IT EVIL INTENT ON A GLOBAL SCALE?
SHA
SHA
DO THE BAD YOKAI STINK FROM THE START?
WHAT ABOUT WHEN THEY'RE *HIDING* THEIR EVIL INTEN-TIONS?
WHAT IF THEY APPROACH YOU NOT MEANING TO KILL YOU, BUT THEN DECIDE THEY WANT TO?
SHA
......
JUNKER-SAN!
WELL ...

GOOD AND EVIL CAN FLIP AROUND QUITE A BIT, DEPENDING ON WHERE YOU'RE LOOKING.
IT WOULD BE COMMON ENOUGH FOR ONE YOU SEE AS GOOD TO BE EVIL TO ME.
SHAA
SHA
ARE YOU TELLING ME TO RISK MY LIFE ON YOUR FLIMSY LOGIC?
EVEN IF YOUR ABILITY REALLY DOES INDICATE WHEN AN NE POSES NO HARM TOWARDS HUMANS...
ARE WE GOING TO CALL YOU UP TO CHECK EVERY SINGLE TIME?
SHA
YOU DON'T HAVE TO LISTEN TO THIS!
DON'T LET HIM CONFUSE YOU, JUNKER-SAN!
ARE YOU GOING TO TRAVEL AROUND THE WORLD SNIFFING NEs?
SHAAAA
EVEN THOUGH AS WE SPEAK...
THERE ARE HUMANS ABOUT TO BE KILLED?
SHA
SHA
JUNKER-SAN!!
SO?!
SHAA
ANSWER ME, PSYCHIC!!!

SHAA

GAH!

KRNKH

GRUNCH...

SHRAAA

...NGH

JUNKER-SAN!

SHAA

YOU CAN'T SAVE ANYONE WITH ARGUMENTS BASED ON EMOTION!

...NGH

...AGH

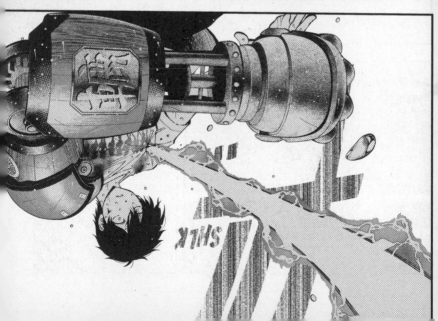

SHLK

NGH
...
SHAAAA
SHA
JUNKER-SAN...
SHA
SHA
MAYBE IT IS...
SHA
AND MAYBE WHAT YOU'RE SAYING IS...
MORE LOGICAL AND RIGHT, IN A WAY.
SHA
AN ARGUMENT BASED ON EMOTION.
BUT ...
ISN'T EMOTION ...
SHAA
WHAT MAKES US HUMAN ?
SHA

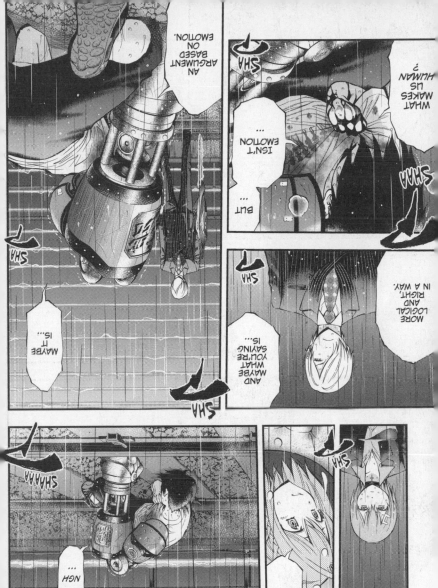

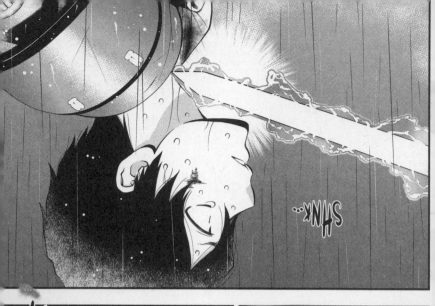

SHK...

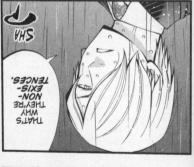

THAT'S WHY THEY'RE NON-EXIS-TENCES.

YOU! WANT TO PUNCH THE PERSON RESPON-SIBLE IN THE FACE!!

SHA

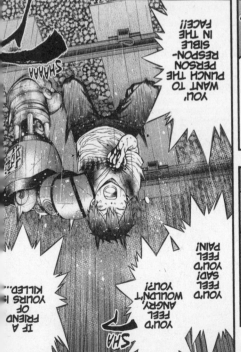

SHAAA

IF A FRIEND OF YOURS IS KILLED...

YOU'D FEEL ANGRY, WOULDN'T YOU?!

YOU'D FEEL SAD! YOU'D FEEL PAIN!

SHA

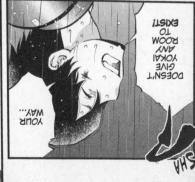

DOESN'T GIVE YOKAI ANY ROOM TO EXIST!

YOUR WAY...

SHA

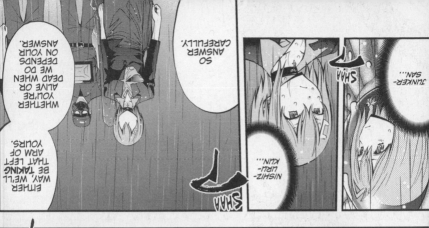

WHETHER YOU'RE ALIVE OR DEAD WHEN WE DO DEPENDS ON YOUR ANSWER.

SO ANSWER CAREFULLY.

EITHER WAY, WE'LL BE TAKING THAT LEFT ARM OF YOURS.

"JUNKER-SAN"....

"NISHIZ-URU-KUN"....

SHAA

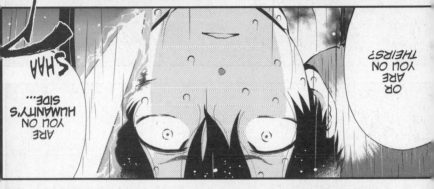

ARE YOU ON HUMANITY'S SIDE....

OR ARE YOU ON THEIRS?

SHAA

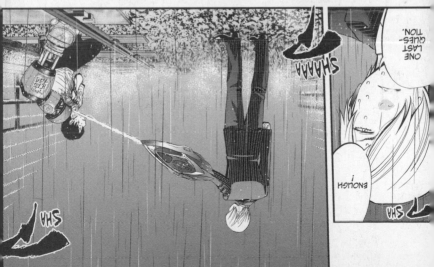

ONE LAST QUES-TION.

ENOUGH!

SHAAAA

SHA

HUMANITY...
SHAAAA
OR YOKAI...
HUMANITY...
OR YOKAI...
I...
E...
SHA
EVEN WITH HUMANS ...
THERE'S BAD PEOPLE...
AND GOOD PEOPLE, TOO!
SHA
AND WITH SPIRITS... THERE'S EVIL ONES, AND GOOD ONES LIKE GUARDIAN SPIRITS!
SHA
SO THEN...

THE YOKAI I KNOW...
ARE ALWAYS THOUGHT-LESS...
ALWAYS SAYING THINGS THAT DON'T MAKE SENSE AND STUFFING THEIR FACES WITH FOOD!
SLUURP!
YOINK
SHA
THEY'RE JEALOUS, AND KINDA DUMB, AND REALLY LAID-BACK!
THEY'RE FULL OF CRAZY ENERGY, NEVER HALF-ASS ANY-THING!
THEY'RE STUPIDLY CHEERFUL ALL THE TIME, BRIGHTENING UP THE WORLD AROUND THEM!
HIDE SEEK
SHAA
THEY'RE ...
GOOD PEOPLE, MORE HUMAN THAN HUMANS THEM-SELVES!
JUNKER-SAN!
SHAA
THAT MEANS...
THERE ARE BAD AND GOOD YOKAI TOO, RIGHT?!
SHAAAAA

AND I WANT TO...
PROTECT ALL OF THESE PEOPLE!
I CAN'T CHOOSE HUMANS OR YOKAI... AND I *WON'T!*
IT'S ALL OF THEM TOGETHER!

MY FRIENDS ARE WHAT'S IMPORTANT TO ME...

AND IT'S THEIR SIDE I'M ON!!!
I SEE.
THEN THIS...
BWOO
IS GOOD-BYE!!
JUNKER-SAN!!

DON
--!!
?!
HE DISA--
LOOK!! ABOVE YOU!!
ROKKA!!
JUNKER-SAN!!

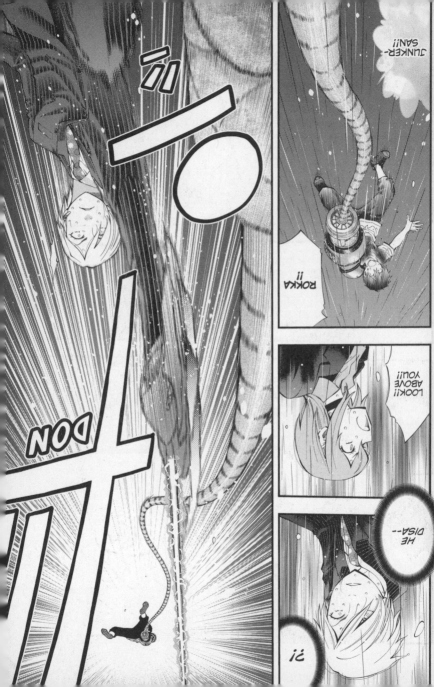

FIGURE IT OUT!!

I'M NOT A ROCKET PUNCH!!

I'M A ROKU-ROKUBI!!

THANKS! YOU SAVED MY BUTT!!

JUNKER-SAN!

HEADBUTT BLITZ WON'T HIT HIM. WHAT SHOULD I DO?

BUT WHAT DO I DO NOW?!

A ROKU-ROKUBI...

WE HAVE TO WORK TOGETHER OR WE WON'T BE ABLE TO SUMMON OUR FULL STRENGTH!!

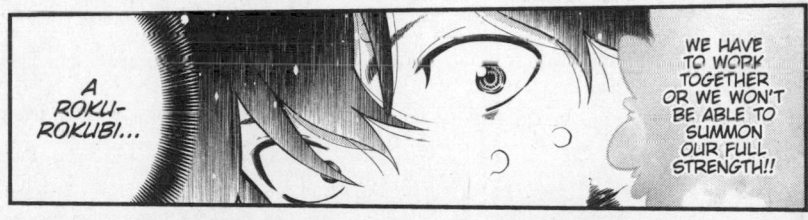

ROKU-ROKUBI...

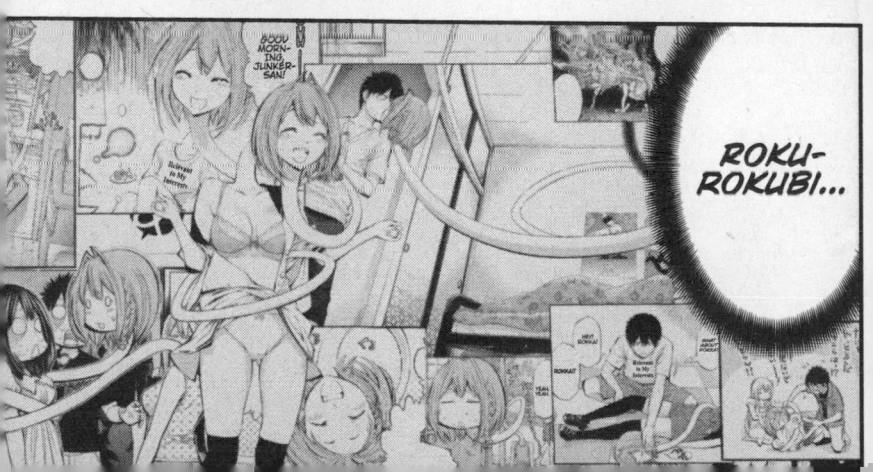

I GET IT!!
SHIIING
I'LL BET EVERY-THING ON...
THIS ONE SHOT!!!
DON
HAA...
超重弩轟砲頭突ッ!!!!!!
HEADBUTT BLITZ!!!!!
FWSH

BWOO
HE...
HE DODGED IT?!
YOU FOOL!
ZWAA
I TOLD YOU THOSE BEELINE ATTACKS AREN'T GOING TO HIT ME!
I'LL TAKE HIM THE MOMENT HE HITS THE GROUND!!
WITH HIS ARM STRETCHED OUT, HE'S DEFENSELESS! HE WON'T BE ABLE TO DO A THING!!
GRIN

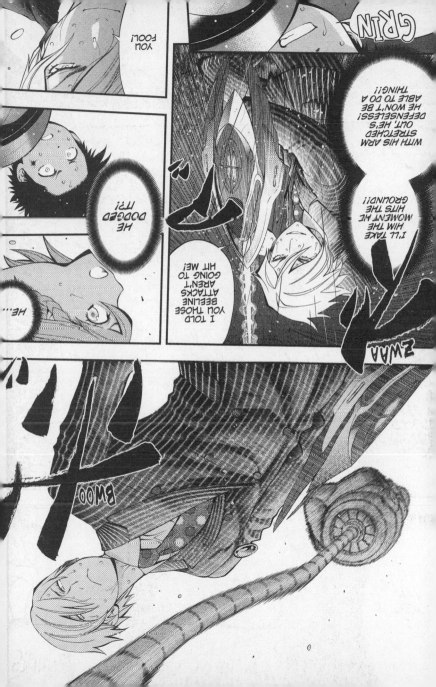

THINK AGAIN, GENIUS!!
HYUU
THAT'S RIGHT!
HYUUHYUN
HYUU
WHY DIDN'T I FIGURE IT OUT BEFORE? ROKKA IS A ROKUROKUBI !!
THIS ISN'T MY FIST! IT'S ROKKA'S HEAD!!
HUH ?!
SPINSPIN
SO THEN...
WHAT ?!
SQUEEZE

PAA!—
!!
SQUEEZE
NYAA!—
WHAT ?!
GWOO
HEY...

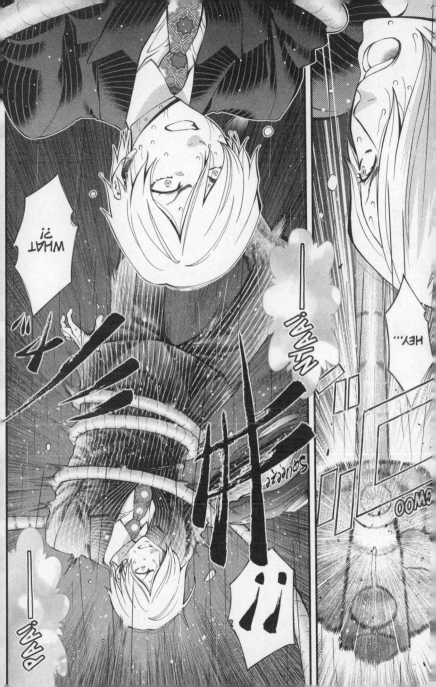

超弩轟縛捕頭突!!!!
HEADBUTT BLITZ!!!!!
NYAN!!!!
ZU-GON

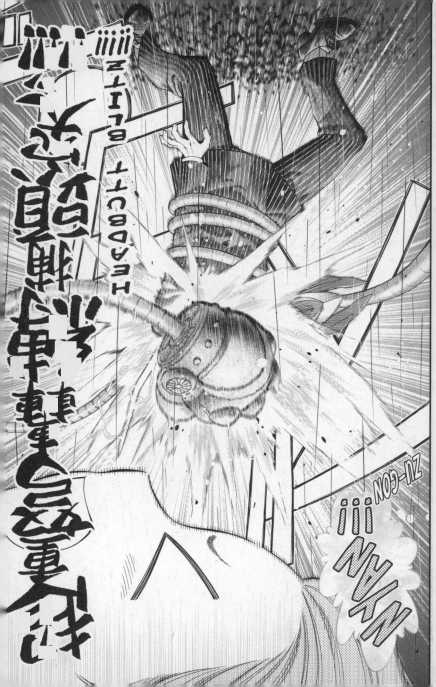

55 A Bridge to Connect! ♪

超重弩轟縛捕頭突ッ!!!!!
HEADBUTT BLITZ!!!!!
PAA!——
NYAA!——
ZU-GON
NYAN!!!
GAH...
AGH!

SHA
SPLAT
SHA
GAH!
TWITCH
TWITCH
......
SHA
HAAH!
HAAH!
SWAY
SHA
NO WAY...
YUKIMURA-SAN IS...
RISE
HAAH...
HAAH...

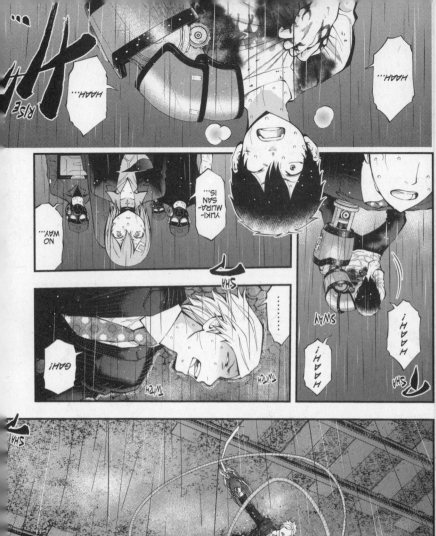

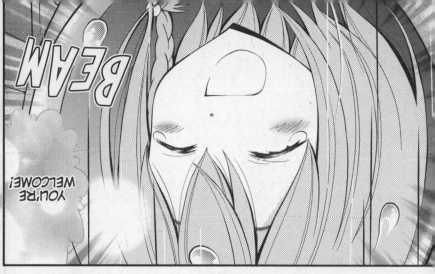

BEAM

YOU'RE WELCOME!

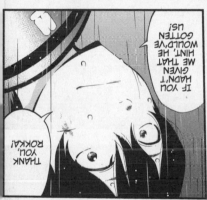

IF YOU HADN'T GIVEN US THAT HINT, WE WOULD'VE GOTTEN US!

THANK YOU, ROKKA!

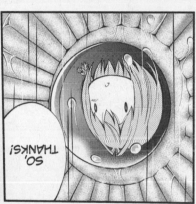

SO, THANKS!

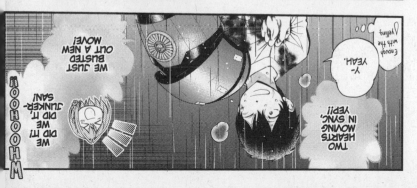

WHOOHOO!

WE DID IT! WE DID IT, JUNKER-SAN!

WE JUST BUSTED OUT A NEW MOVE!

Enough with the yelling.

Y-YEAH.

TWO HEARTS MOVING IN SYNC, YEP!!

SHAAAA
TURN
!
SHA
URK!
CRUNCH
SHA
CRUNCH
CRUNCH
CRUNCH...
SHA
SHA
CLACK
SHA
CLONK

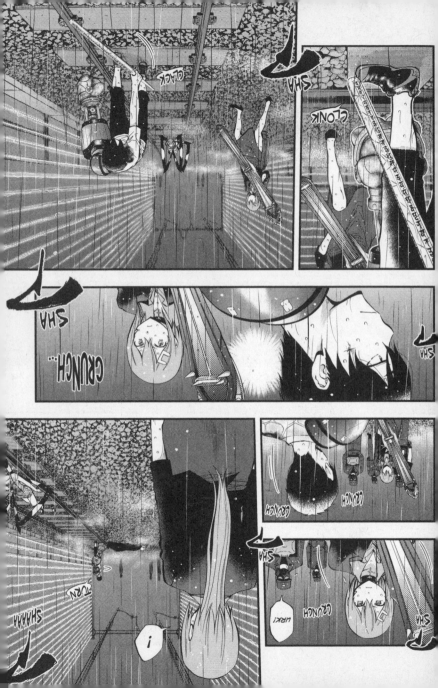

SHA
SHAAAA
HIME-CHAN...
SHA
LIFT
SHA
CRUNCH
STOP RIGHT THERE!
KLING
SHING
SHAA
FWSH FWSH

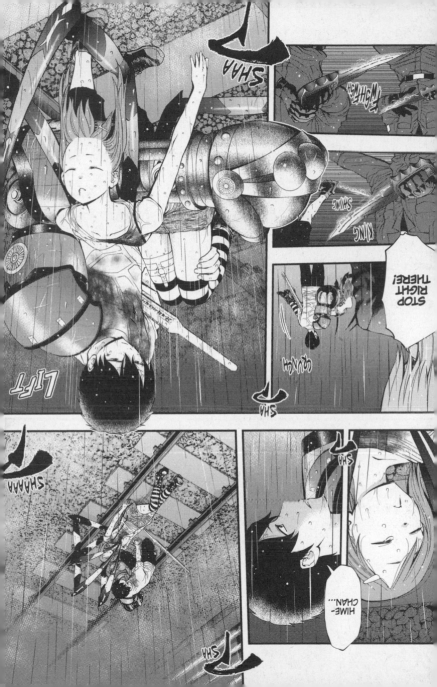

YOU THINK YOU CAN JUST WALK AWAY?!
SHAAAA
SHA
SHA
......
WHY, HOU-JOU-SAN?
SHA
YOU THINK YOU CAN STOP ME?
SHA
......
SHA

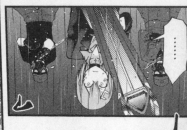

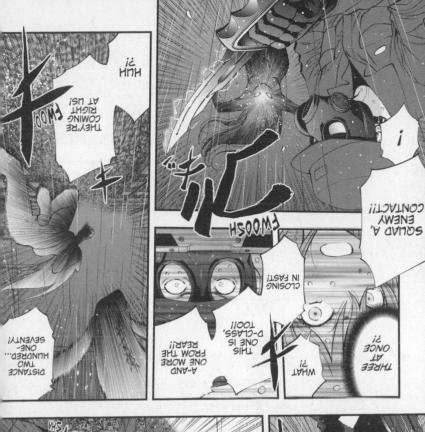

HUH？！

THEY'RE COMING RIGHT AT US!

FWOOM

SQUAD A, ENEMY CONTACT!!

CLOSING IN FAST!

THIS ONE IS D-CLASS, TOO!!

A-AND ONE MORE FROM THE REAR!!

DISTANCE TWO HUNDRED... ONE-SEVENTY!

FWOOSH

WHAT？！

THREE AT ONCE？！

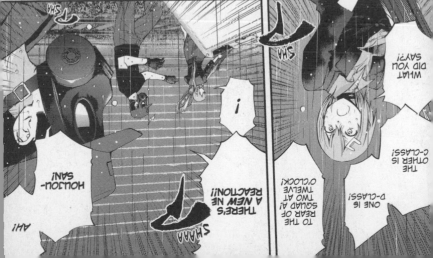

WHAT DID YOU SAY?！

THE OTHER IS C-CLASS!

ONE IS D-CLASS!

TO THE REAR OF SQUAD A! TWO AT TWELVE O'CLOCK!

THERE'S A NEW NE REACTION!!

SHAAA

HOUJOU-SAN!

AH!

BWOO
ERK!
HYUN
PA-WHAM!!
SHWOO
WHA ...?
HYUU...
SUPAAAN
SLICE!!
GON!!

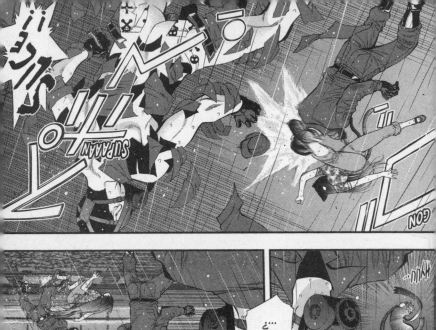

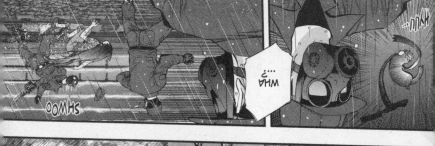

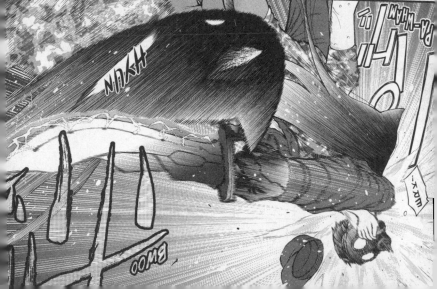

HUH?!
SHWOO
HUH ?!
MY CLOTHES !
DON'T WORRY. WE SHAN'T HURT YOU TOO BADLY!
GURAA
?!
NURI!!
ZUSHAAN
GYAAH!!
WHAT ?
NO WAY...
IN JUST AN INSTANT ...

CRUNCH
!
SHAAAA
H-HOLD IT RIGHT THERE!!
YOU REALLY WANT TO MAKE *ME* YOUR ENEMY?!
SHAA
......
I...
SHA
DON'T THINK OF YOU AS MY ENEMY.
BUT MY FRIENDS MEAN A LOT TO ME.
SHAA
AND *IF* YOU TRY TO HURT THEM AGAIN...

I'LL FIGHT WITH ALL MY STRENGTH ...
SHAAAA
TO PROTECT THEM!!
SHA
IF YOU GUYS SAY YOU'RE GONNA HUNT YOKAI FOR HUMANITY...
THEN I...
WILL BE THERE FOR BOTH HUMANS...
AND YOKAI.

I'LL BE THERE AS A BRIDGE TO CONNECT THEM BOTH!!
SHAAA
SHAA

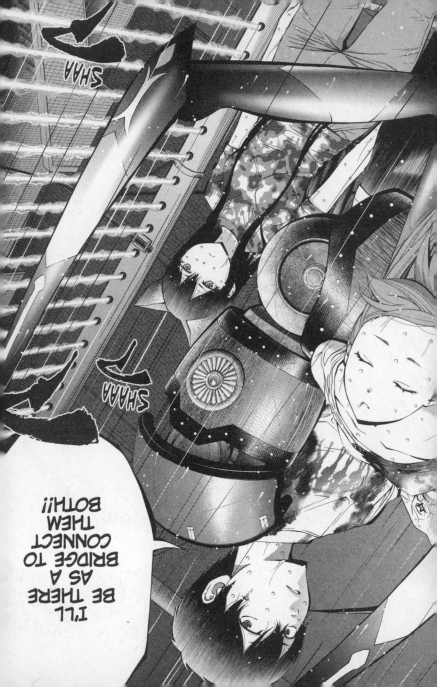

SHAAAAA

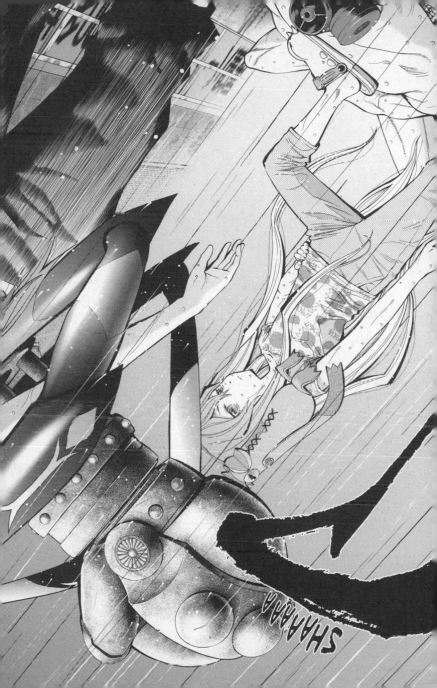

NISHIZ-URU...
YATSU-KI...
SHA
JUST...
WHAT...
ON EARTH ARE YOU?!
SHA
TUNK...
SHA

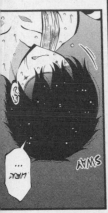

...GRK...

SWAY

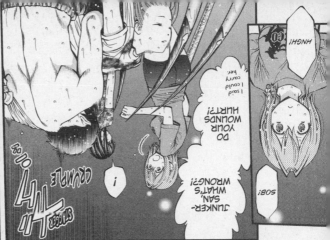

HNGH!

SOB!

JUNKER-SAN, WHAT'S WRONG?!

DO YOUR WOUNDS HURT?!

I said I could carry her.

STAGGER 4 GRUMBLE

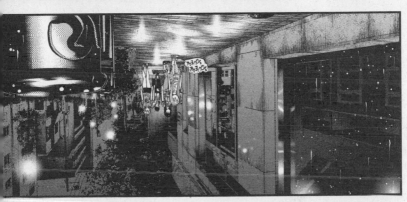

SQUELCH SQUELCH

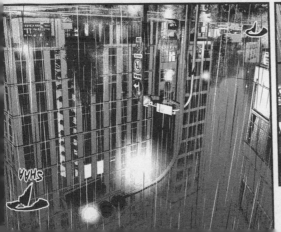

SHAA

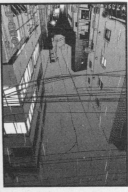

SHAA

"PROTECT THEM"?
"FIGHT WITH...
ALL MY STRENGTH"?
I'M SO FULL OF IT!!
I COULDN'T PROTECT HER!
HIC!
I COULDN'T EVEN PROTECT THE ONE PERSON IN FRONT OF ME...
HOW CAN I TALK ABOUT PROTECTING ANYONE?!
WHAT WAS THAT BULLSHIT ABOUT BEING A BRIDGE?!
SORRY...
!
JUNKER-SAN...
SORRY, HIME-CHAN.
I'M SORRY... I'M SORRY!!

I THINK THEY CALL IT...
THANATOSIS?
HUH?
!
JUNKER-SAN!!
IT'S WHEN SPIDERS...
FEIGN DEATH!

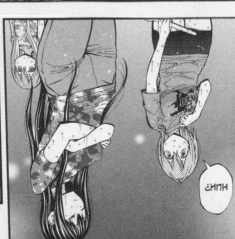

YA...
TSUKI...

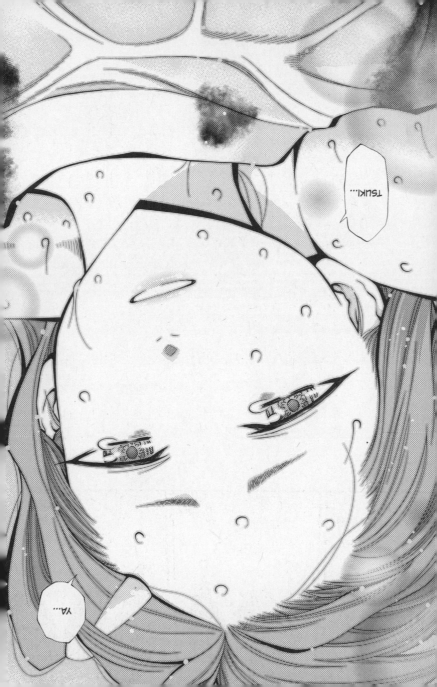

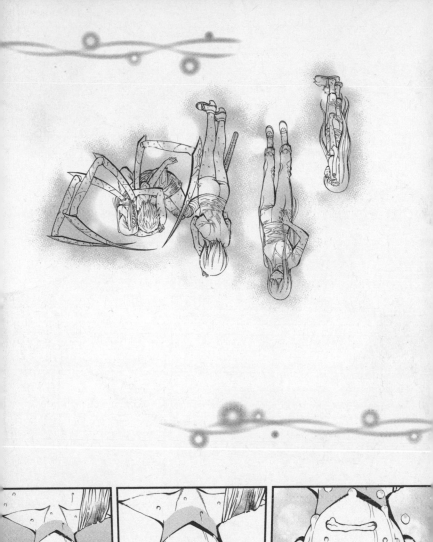

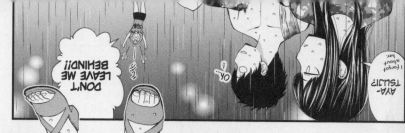

DON'T LEAVE ME BEHIND!!

Oh...

AYA-TSUJI!?

I forgot about her.

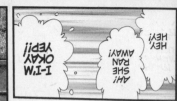

AH! SHE RAN AWAY!

HEY! HEY!

I-I'M OKAY YEP!!

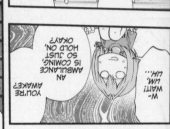

W-WAIT! UM... UH...

YOU'RE AWAKE?

AN AMBULANCE IS COMING, SO JUST HOLD ON, OKAY?

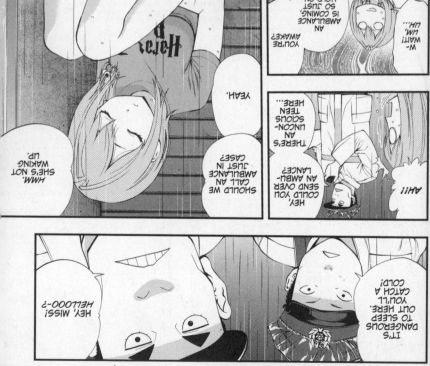

HMM, SHE'S NOT WAKING UP.

YEAH.

SHOULD WE CALL AN AMBULANCE JUST IN CASE?

HEY, COULD YOU SEND OVER AN AMBU-LANCE?

THERE'S AN UNCON-SCIOUS TEEN HERE...

AH!

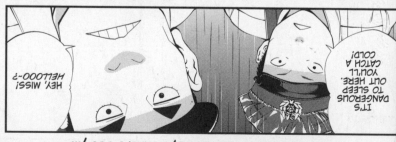

HEY, MISS! HELLOOO~?

IT'S DANGEROUS TO SLEEP OUT HERE. YOU'LL CATCH A COLD!

Extra comic: Meanwhile, Rokka's body...

YATSUKI... ♡
AHH, YEAH!! ♡
56 Sudden Visitor! ♪
WH-WHY ARE YOU NAKED?
WAIT, ME, TOO?! HUH?! WHAT?!
ACK!
HEY...
THIS TIME, LET'S HAVE A...
REAL MATCH. ♡
HUH?! WH-WHAT DO YOU MEAN, "REAL"?!
LET ME SUCK YOU. ♡
S-S-SUCK?! HUH?! HEY! HOLD ON...
WHOA! YOU CAN'T DO THAT.
SLURP SLURP
Haah!
SHOOOP
LICK LICK
SUCK
AH! NOT...
OHHH...
N-NOT THERE...

MORE!!
AHHH!♥
Haah!
Haah!
56
Sudden Visitor! ♪

......

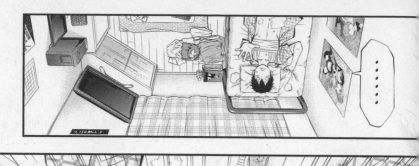

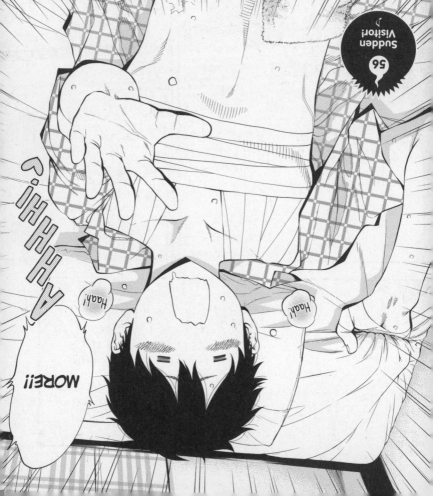

MY ROOM ...?
IT WAS A DREAM...
ARGH! WISH I HADN'T WOKEN UP!
It was just getting good!
......
SO BY "MORE"... HE MEANT HERE, TOO, RIGHT?
I-IT'S KINDA GOTTEN BIGGER, THOUGH.
BA-THUMP BA-THUMP
BA-THUMP BA-THUMP
TUG TUG
WAAGH!!!!
LEAP
YEEK!
WHAT ARE YOU DOING ?!
TILT
DA-DON
AH!
GYAAAH!!

OWIE...
PUSSY SHOT!♥
UH!
YOU'RE THE WORST!
HMPH!
YOU WERE ASLEEP SO LONG, I FIGURED YOU'D SMELL GROSS, SO I WAS WIPING YOU DOWN!
AND YOU SUDDENLY GET A HARD-ON!
YOU SAID "MORE," SO I KEPT GOING!
I-I WASN'T SAYING IT TO YOU!
OW!
THEN WHO WERE YOU TALKING TO?!
TH-THAT'S NOT IMPORTANT!!
NYAAAAAAGH!
WAAAGH!
S-SORRY!

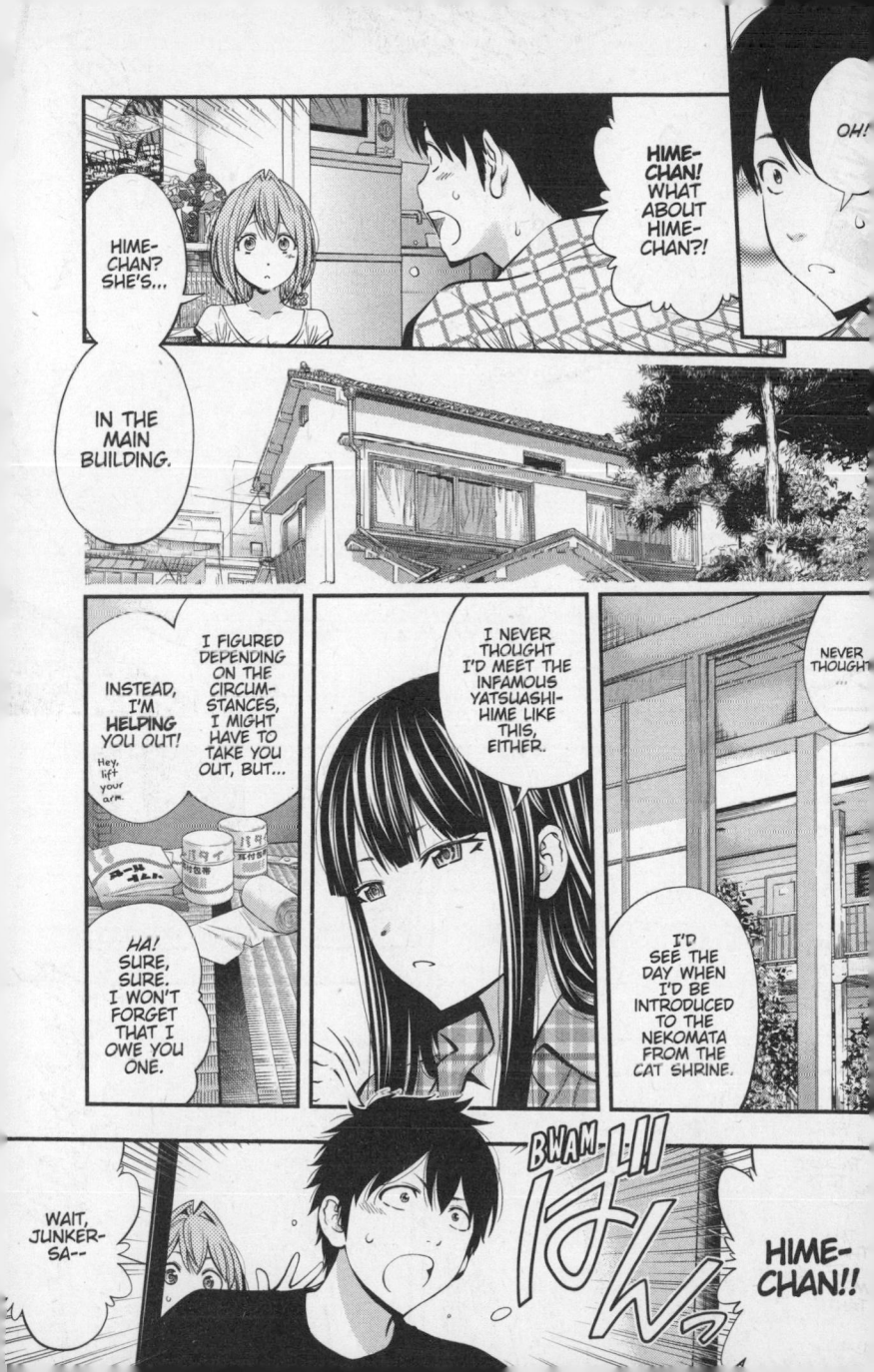

HIME-CHAN? SHE'S...

HIME-CHAN! WHAT ABOUT HIME-CHAN?!

OH!

IN THE MAIN BUILDING.

INSTEAD, I'M **HELPING** YOU OUT!

Hey, lift your arm.

I FIGURED DEPENDING ON THE CIRCUM-STANCES, I MIGHT HAVE TO TAKE YOU OUT, BUT...

I NEVER THOUGHT I'D MEET THE INFAMOUS YATSUASHI-HIME LIKE THIS, EITHER.

NEVER THOUGHT...

HA! SURE, SURE. I WON'T FORGET THAT I OWE YOU ONE.

I'D SEE THE DAY WHEN I'D BE INTRODUCED TO THE NEKOMATA FROM THE CAT SHRINE.

WAIT, JUNKER-SA--

BWAM--!!

HIME-CHAN!!

AH!
EEEEK!!!
ACK! S-S-S-SORRY!!
JEEZ, JUNKER-SAN!!
DID YOU DO THAT ON PUR-POSE?
N-NO! I DIDN'T MEAN TO! I SWEAR ...
HEY... WHEN IT HAPPENED ...
ALONG WITH THE PAIN, SOME MYSTE-RIOUS THING...
LIKE A POWER OVER-FLOWING WITH LIFE FORCE, FLOWED INTO ME.
AND IT FELT AS IF IT WERE ACTUALLY COMING FROM YOU.
THAT'S HOW I MANAGED TO SURVIVE, I THINK.

THANK YOU FOR SAVING ME!
IF YOU HADN'T BEEN THERE...
I WOULD HAVE DIED FOR SURE.
I DIDN'T REALLY...
......
THOSE GCUP PEOPLE...
ARE DANGER-OUS.
PROTECT EVERY-ONE...
OKAY?
YEAH!
I WILL!
SO...
GET SOME SLEEP, ALL RIGHT?
YEAH.

GUYS! LISTEN!!
BWAM
BOOOOOOTY!!
STRETCH

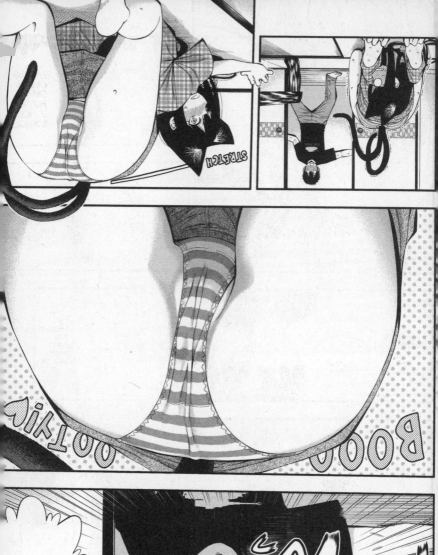

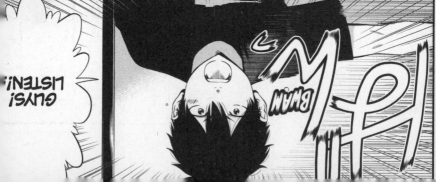

WE'RE BAAAACK! ♪
WE WENT TO GET ICE CREAM! ♡
CRUNCH CRUNCH
'Tis hot out.
HIDE AND SEEK
GORIGORI-KUN
WAS THAT ON PURPOSE?
I REALLY DIDN'T MEAN TO. I'M SORRY...
He saw me.
POP
HUH? WHAT HAPPENED HERE?
She's gone all red too.
Your face is bright red, Junker-san.
ANYWAY! MORE IMPORTANTLY, LISTEN TO THIS!
WHAT, WHAT?!
OH, NO...
NOT YOU, NANAO. LEAVE THE ROOM FOR A MINUTE, 'K?
WIBBLE
SORRY.
PLIP
PLIP
PLIP
WAHHH!
YOU'RE A JERK, ONIICHAN!!
YOU PRE-MATURELY-EJACULATING LOSER!!
HUH?!
You made her cry!
You made her cry!
I'm gonna go tell the teacher!
ROKKA! DON'T TEACH NANAO WEIRD STUFF!!
HIDE

I TOLD THEM ABOUT EVERYTHING THAT HAD HAPPENED...
IN THAT BATTLE OVER THE CHUO LINE.
I'LL BE THERE AS A BRIDGE TO CONNECT THEM BOTH!!
AND HOW I MADE ENEMIES OF THE ORGANIZATION...
ZERO!
ZERO...
YOUR SINS!!
HOW HOUJOU-SAN TRIED TO RECRUIT ME, AND HOW I RAN INTO HIME-CHAN AGAIN...
GO ON ANOTHER DATE WITH ME?
THEN I TOLD THEM...
AND HOW BECAUSE OF THAT, I LOST A CHANCE TO GET SOME INFORMATION ABOUT RETURNING NANAO TO HER BODY.
I TOLD THEM ALL I KNEW ABOUT GCUP...
THIS IS OUR MISSION AT GCUP!

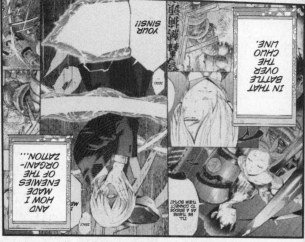

ABOUT THE DANGER WE'RE IN.
GCUP PROBABLY KNOWS WHERE I LIVE.
I'M SURE THEY KNOW ABOUT NIA-CHAN, ICCHAN, AND THE HINNAGAMI.
THEY COULD ATTACK US AT ANY TIME.
BUT...
BUT I'LL MAKE SURE TO KEEP YOU...
ALL...
SAFE ...
I...
BLUSH
SWEAR.
WHAT ?!
I COULDN'T HEAR YOU! SPEAK LOUDER!
HE'S PRACTI-CALLY WHISPER-ING!

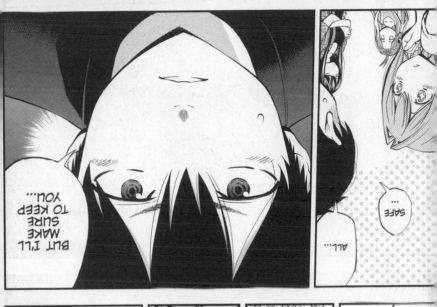

HMPH
PROTECTION?
GUESS THEY HEARD IT.
AS IF I NEED THAT!
BESIDES, YOU'VE ALREADY SAVED ME ONCE!
IT'S MY TURN TO SAVE YOU!
NIA-CHAN...
YEP, SHE'S RIGHT!
DON'T GET YOURSELF SO WORKED UP ABOUT THIS!
IT'S THE SAME AS USUAL!
JUST KEEP BEING YOUR LOSERY AND OCCASIONALLY COOL SELF, JUNKER-SAN!
ROKKA ...
YOU STILL THINK I'M A LOSER?
AH! NO! I MEAN, JUST IN DAILY LIFE, YOU KNOW?
SO HE WAS WORRIED ABOUT THAT.

SEE HERE...
!
WHAT'S BEEN SAID CANNOT BE UNSAID, YOU KNOW?
WE'LL TRUST IN YOU, LAD!
BECAUSE I KNOW YOU SHALL BE...

SHRINE
HIDE SEEK
OFFERINGS
THAT BRIDGE YOU SPOKE OF!!

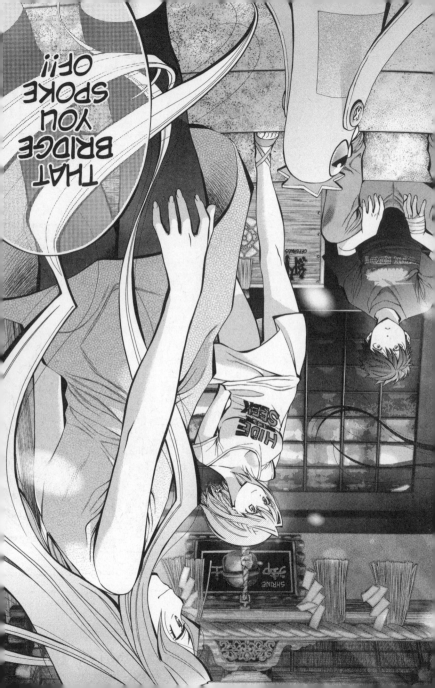

I WILL!

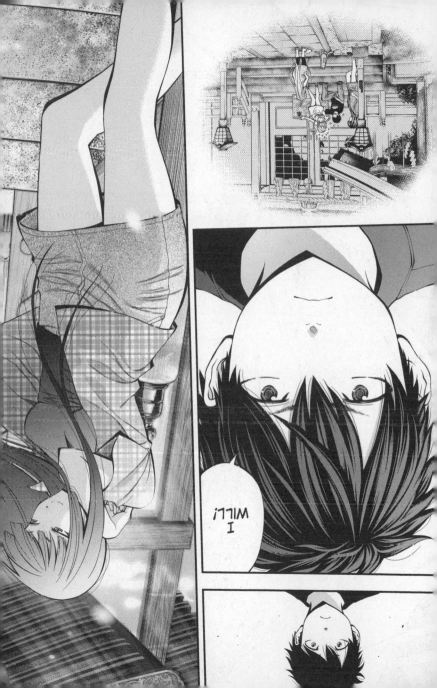

HEY...
CAN I ASK YOU SOMETHING?
Wow, Kappa-chan!
What?!
SLICE!
NAKED
HM?

IF...
IF I END UP LIKE HIME-CHAN DID THE OTHER DAY...

WOULD YOU...
CRY LIKE THAT FOR ME?
TANK ROAD!!

HUH
WHAT ARE YOU BABBLING AB--
!
STARE
!
JERK
NGH!
HEY?! SO, WOULD YOU?!
ANSWER ME!
GRAB
YOU DUM--
HEY! DON'T SMOOSH ME LIKE THAT, YOU JERK!
HER BOOBS!
TELL ME!

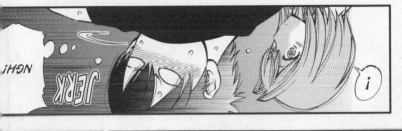

ANSWER ME ALREADY!

HER BOOBS...

THEY'RE ON MY SHOULDER!!

もっちゅ SMOOOOOSH ーーん

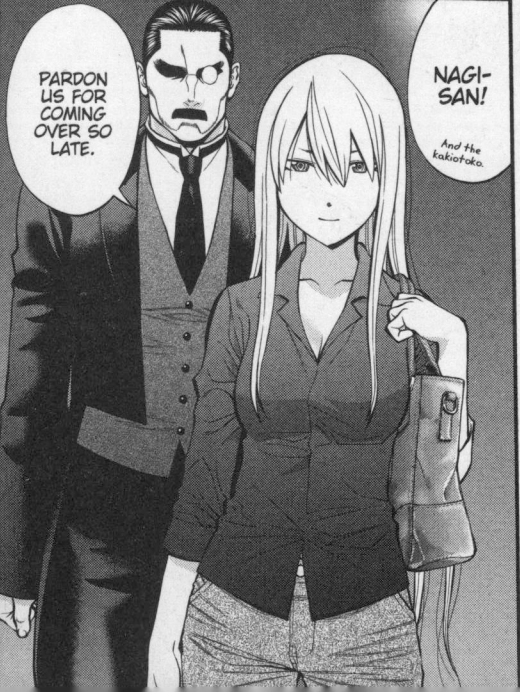

PARDON US FOR COMING OVER SO LATE.

NAGI-SAN!

And the kakiotoko.

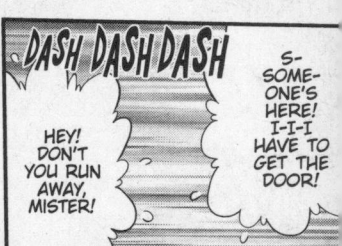

DASH DASH DASH

HEY! DON'T YOU RUN AWAY, MISTER!

S-SOMEONE'S HERE! I-I-I HAVE TO GET THE DOOR!

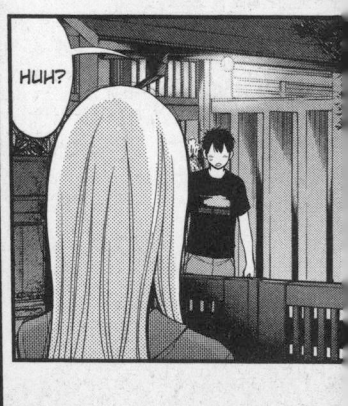

HUH?

WHAT'S GOING ON?
CREAK
THERE'S SOMEONE I'D LIKE YOU TO MEET.
THIS WAS THE ONLY TIME HE COULD COME SEE YOU.

LET ME INTRO-DUCE YOU...

TO MAKURA-GAESHI-KUN!
!!

57
The Path of Souls! ♪

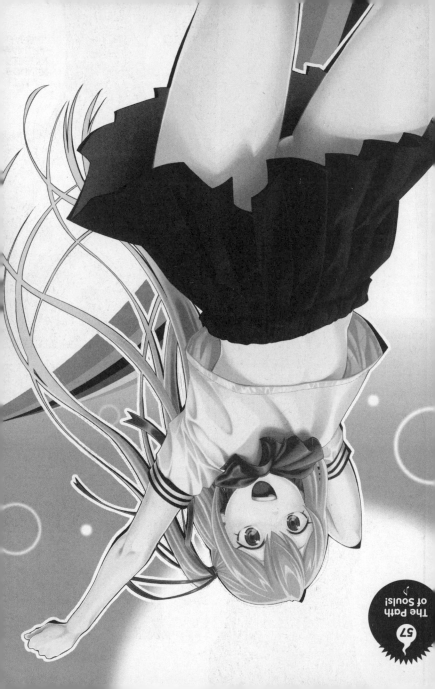

A MAKURA-GAESHI?!
THIS KID?!
"THIS KID"? WHAT A RUDE HUMAN!
AH! SORRY.
MAKURA-ZAKI RISAI.
I'M A SOUNEN RISSHIN MAKURA-GAESHI.

According to folklore, the soul exits the body during dreams. If the pillow is turned over while the person is dreaming, it is believed that the soul can't return to the body. Because of this, tales also describe the makuragaeshi as a yokai to be feared, and as takers of life.

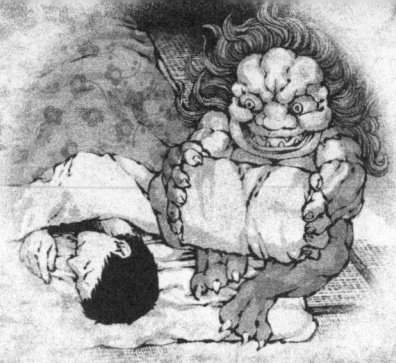

MAKURAGAESHI

Stories of this yokai are told across Japan. The term means "turning the pillow," or it can also be written with characters meaning "anti-pillow." The creature comes to sleeping people at night and flips over their pillows, or flips the person around so their head points in a different direction. It is thought to be a mischievous yokai that takes the form of a child, usually a young boy.

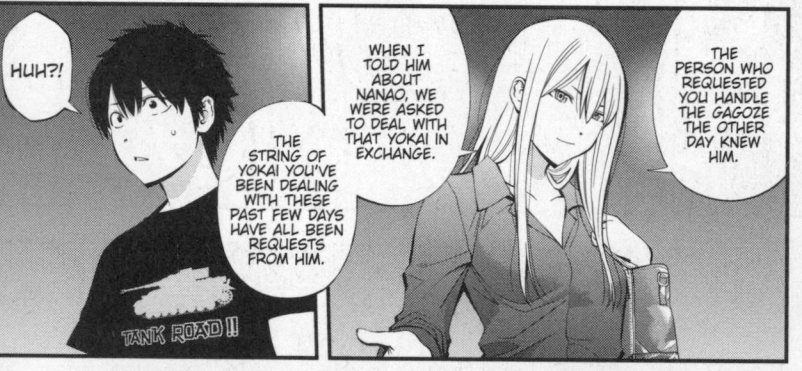

HUH?!

THE STRING OF YOKAI YOU'VE BEEN DEALING WITH THESE PAST FEW DAYS HAVE ALL BEEN REQUESTS FROM HIM.

WHEN I TOLD HIM ABOUT NANAO, WE WERE ASKED TO DEAL WITH THAT YOKAI IN EXCHANGE.

THE PERSON WHO REQUESTED YOU HANDLE THE GAGOZE THE OTHER DAY KNEW HIM.

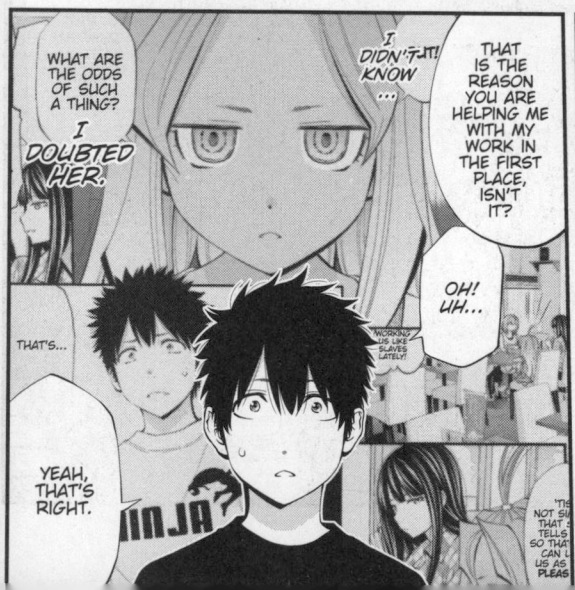

WHAT ARE THE ODDS OF SUCH A THING?

I DOUBTED HER.

I DIDN'T KNOW...

THAT IS THE REASON YOU ARE HELPING ME WITH MY WORK IN THE FIRST PLACE, ISN'T IT?

OH! UH...

THAT'S...

YEAH, THAT'S RIGHT.

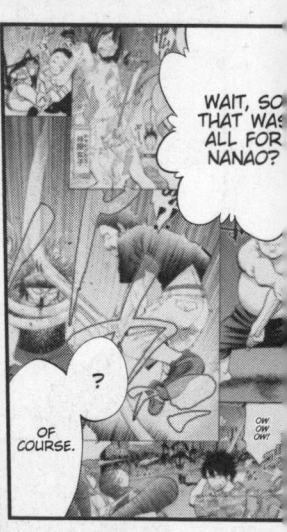

WAIT, SO THAT WAS ALL FOR NANAO?

?

OF COURSE.

OW OW OW!

I'M SORRY!!
ACK! YOU STARTLED ME!
WHAT'S WRONG?
BOW
EVEN IF I DIDN'T KNOW, I--
!
WAIT...
WHERE'D MAKURA-GAESHI-KUN GO?
HM?
HUH?!
WAFT...
!
THAT STINKS!!
IT COULDN'T BE...?!
YOU'RE ...
FAST ASLEEP, AREN'T YOU?

KEEP ON SLEEPING... DEEPER.
SNORE
SLIDE...
FALL INTO ETERNAL SLUMBER.
SHING
SEVER THE SOUL PERFECTLY...
AND TURN OVER THE PIL--
YARGH!!!
THWACK
DON'T KILL MY GRAMPA!!
OW.
YOU CAN DO ETHEREAL ATTACKS WITH YOUR BARE HANDS?
Not bad.
NAGI-SAN! HE STINKS!
He's a bad yokai!
THMP
HE'S HEARING YOUR REQUEST. YOU CAN IGNORE THE *LITTLE THINGS* IN LIGHT OF THAT.
"LITTLE THINGS"? YOU CALL THIS A "LITTLE THING"?!

!
WAIT...
WHY IS YATSUASHI-HIME HERE?
I'LL EXPLAIN LATER.
It's a long story.
A MAKURA-GAESHI?!
THIS SPROG?!
I DON'T WANT TO HEAR A LITTLE BRAT CALLING ME A "SPROG."
WATCH YOUR TONGUE !!
......
WHAT IS THIS PLACE, A YOKAI FLOP-HOUSE?
Lame.
AREN'T THERE ANY HUMANS HERE? COME ON.
IF THERE ARE, WHAT'RE YOU PLANNING TO DO WITH THEM?

?
FUWA
SO, IT'S HER.
SO? YOU THINK YOU CAN PUT HER BACK?
......
I CAN'T... OR RATHER, I DON'T WANT TO.
WHY NOT?! WHAT DO YOU MEAN?!
BECAUSE SHE'S TOTALLY MY TYPE!
WHAT A HORN DOG!!
With a totally straight face, too!

IF YOU GO BACK TO YOUR BODY, TIME WILL MAKE YOUR FLESH SAG AND YOU'LL GET ALL WRINKLY AND UGLY.
WOULDN'T YOU RATHER BE BEAUTIFUL LIKE YOU ARE NOW, FOREVER?
?
HEY !!!
What are you saying?!
THEN HOW ABOUT PUTTING YOU BACK IN YOUR BODY FOR NOW, AND DIVORCING IT FROM YOU AGAIN LATER?
HOW ABOUT OTHING, YOU LITTLE SHIT!!!
on't just casually take her hands!!
Divorce ...?
!
HER SPIRITUAL POWER IS WEAK.
HEY, CAN YOU TOUCH OBJECTS?
HUH?
NO, I CAN'T.
I THOUGHT SO.
......
WHAT ?
I COULD DO IT.
REALLY ?!
BUT MOST LIKELY...

ALL I DO IS CREATE A PATH TO CONNECT THE BODY AND SOUL.
WHAT ?!
WHETHER OR NOT THE PERSON CAN STRUGGLE THROUGH...
THE VARIOUS DIFFICULTIES AND BARRIERS THAT AWAIT THEM IS UP TO THEM.
WITH HER FAINT SPIRITUAL POWER, I DOUBT SHE'D EVEN BE ABLE TO REACH HER BODY.
I CAN GET BACK TO MY BODY?!
IT'D BE POINTLESS.
NANAO ...
IT'S IMPOSSIBLE FOR HER!
?!
TANK ROAD !!

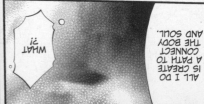

NANAO WANTS TO EAT TOGETHER WITH YOU GUYS, AND GO TO SCHOOL WITH YOU GUYS!
NANAO WANTS TO LIVE TOGETHER WITH YOU!!
NANAO WILL DO IT!!
NANAO...
PLEASE ...
......
WHAT-EVER.

WELL?
READY?
HAAH...
SLIDE
PHEW!
CONNECT THE SOUL PERFECT-LY...
KRIIIN

SLIDE
NOW...
HAVE A NICE TRIP.
AND TURN OVER TH PILLO !!!
FLIP
THAT'S ...

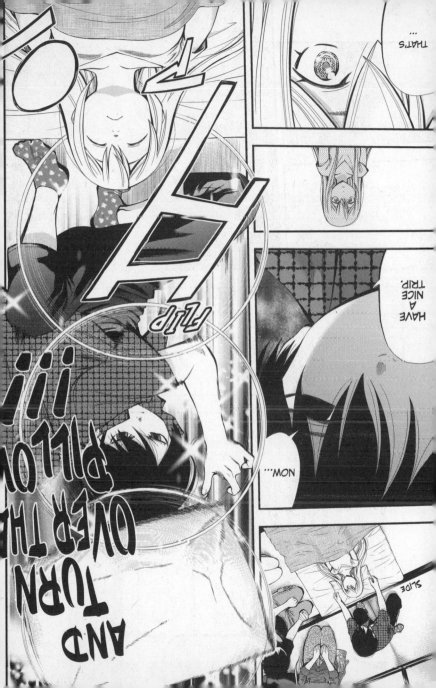

THE PATH OF SOULS!

WHAT...
IS THIS PLACE?

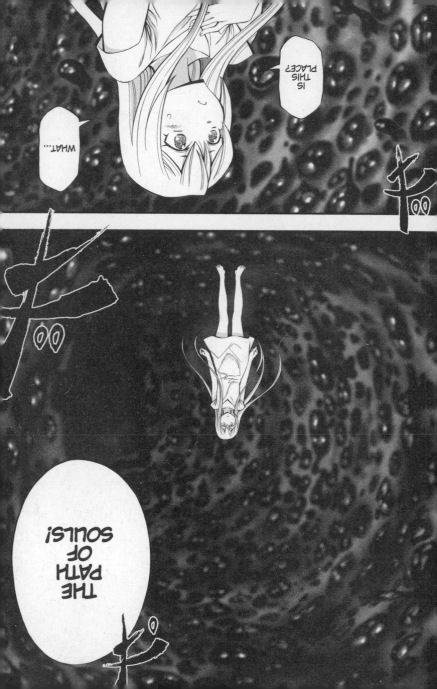

オooo
IF YOU WANT TO LEAVE THAT PLACE, TELL ME.
I CAN GET YOU OUT IMMEDIATELY.
PLEASE TRY NOT TO PUSH YOURSELF TOO FAR, OR ELSE YOU MAY END UP BEING EATEN BY A MALICIOUS SPIRIT.
WH-WHAT'S ...
GOING ON?

WANT TO SEE?
I CAN LOOK ?!
GWOOO
THERE SHE IS!!
LOOK, NAGI-SAN!!
NANA-CHAN!!
WHAT IS THAT PLACE?!
How loathsome!!
URK ...
I'M SCARED, ONII-CHAN.
YOU CAN DO IT, NANAO!
PAN-YANYAN, NANA-CHAN!
YOU'RE GOING TO GET BACK TO YOUR BODY!
......

STEP
FREEZE
......
THAT'S IT! YOU CAN TAKE IT SLOW!
TAKE YOUR TIME. JUST KEEP ON MOVING FORWARD!
......
JOLT
EEK!!
SHLOOP

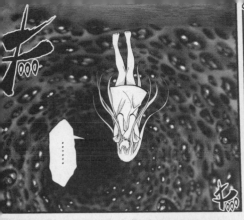

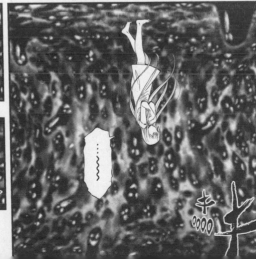

WHAT...
IS THIS?
A POND?
A POND?!
WHAT THE HELL?! YOU MEAN SHE HAS TO SWIM?!
IT'S OKAY. IT'S SHALLOW.
WELL ...
TO BE HONEST, IT'S NOT JUST A POND.
......
WHAT IS THIS?
IT'S LIKE JELLY ...
SPLRCH
IT'S ALL SLIPPERY AND HARD TO WALK THROUGH ...
SQUISH

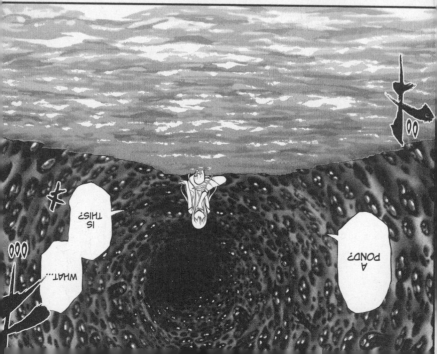

SHUDDER SHUDDER
SHUDDER SHUDDER
SHUDDER
!
EEK!!
BLOOSH
!!!
ぐはあっ
AH...
GROPE
AH!
GROPE GROPE
GROPE
NOOO! WHAT IS THIS?!
IT'S GROSS !!
GROPE
GROPE
HEY! WHAT THE HELL IS THAT STUFF ?!
THIS IS... YOU KNOW
BURBLE
MY CLOTHES!
BURBLE
BURBLE, BURBLE
YEAH.

IT'S SLIME THAT ONLY MELTS CLOTHING!
BURBLE
BURBLE
BURBLE
BURBLE
BURBLE
NOOO!!!
ARE YOU KIDDING ME?!!
DU-DUUN

THIS STUFF SHOWS UP A LOT IN PORN GAMES.
OH, THAT STUFF!
TUMP
DON'T LOOK SO HAPPY!!!

58
Fighting as Her Brother! ♪
IT'S SLIME THAT ONLY MELTS CLOTHING!
NOOO!!!
GROPE
BURBLE
ARE YOU KIDDING ME?!!
GROPE
どどどーーーん
DU-DUUUN
BURBLE
BURBLE
BURBLE
GROPE

WHAT IS THIS? IT'S SO GROSS!
OOZE
GROPE
BURBLE
BURBLE
BURBLE
IT'S EATING UP MY CLOTHES!
GROPE
BURBLE
NOOO!
OOZE
BURBLE
OOZE

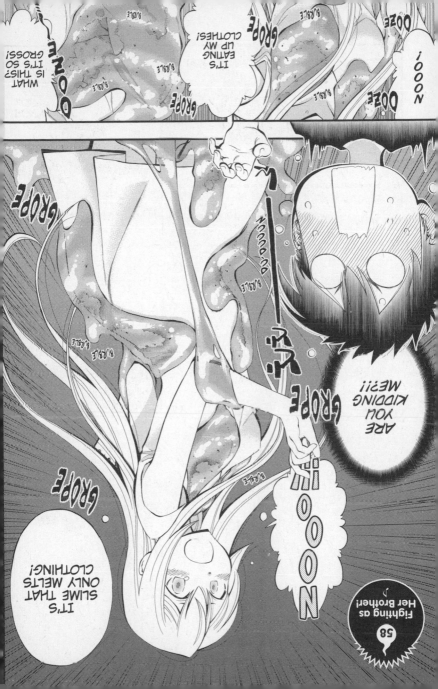

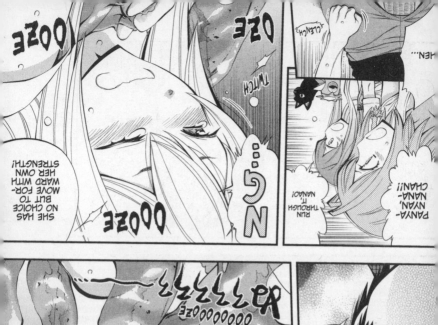

SHE HAS NO CHOICE BUT TO MOVE FOR-WARD WITH HER OWN STRENGTH!

OOZE

OOZE

OOZE

TWITCH

...EH!

CLENCH

RUN THROUGH IT, NANAO!

NYAN, NANA-CHAN!!

PANYA~ NYAN, NANA-

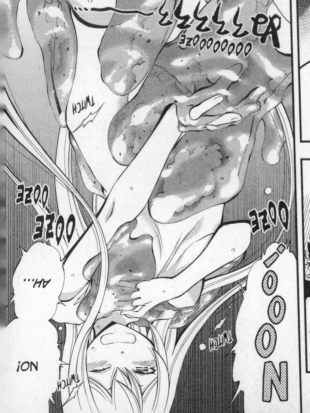

EzOOOOOOOO

TWITCH

OOZE

AH...

OOZE

NO!

TWITCH

TWITCH

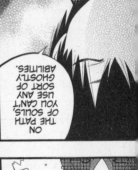

ON THE PATH OF SOULS, YOU CAN'T USE ANY SORT OF GHOSTLY ABILITIES.

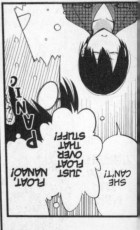

PANIC

JUST FLOAT OVER THAT STUFF!

FLOAT, NANAO!

SHE CAN'T!

THEN PUT ME IN THERE!!
SEND MY SOUL TO WHERE NANAO'S IS!
WHAT ?!
WAIT, WAIT, WAIT! THIS IS NANAO'S STRUGGLE!
WHAT POINT WOULD THERE BE IN YOUR GOING?!
MY LITTLE SISTER IS IN TROUBLE! I CAN'T JUST SIT HERE TWIDDLING MY THUMBS!!
TANK ROAD!!
SILENCE IS ALSO A BROTHER'S PART! DON'T YOU HAVE FAITH IN NANAO?!
IT'S NOT ABOUT FAITH!
......
ADVANCED BRANCHES OF PILLOW-TURNING INCLUDE TECHNIQUES TO SUBSTITUTE SOULS.
SINCE THAT'S POSSIBLE, IT MUST ALSO BE POSSIBLE TO SEND A THIRD PARTY INTO ANOTHER PERSON'S PATH OF SOULS.
THEN ...!
BUT YOU DO UNDER-STAND...
YOU'LL ESSEN-TIALLY BE...

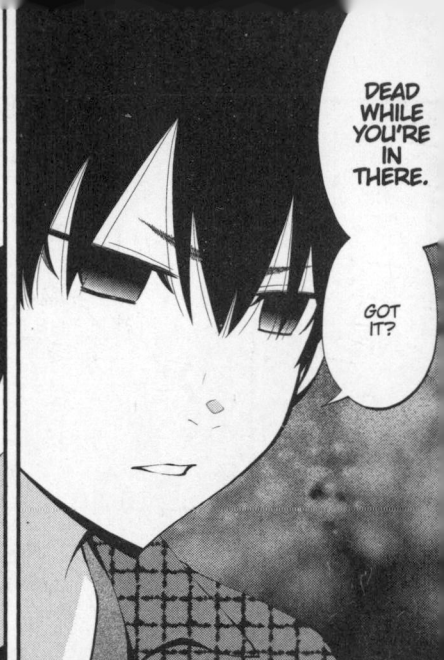

ONCE IT'S ALL DONE, YOU'LL PUT ME BACK, RIGHT?

DEAD WHILE YOU'RE IN THERE.

GOT IT?

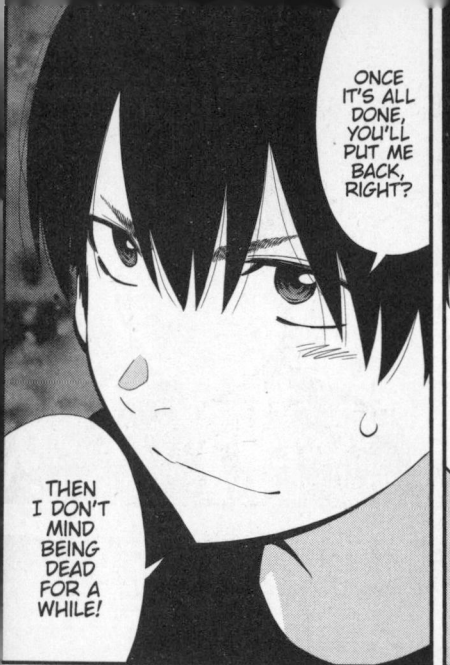

THEN I DON'T MIND BEING DEAD FOR A WHILE!

HE SURE HAS SOME EXCEPTIONAL DETERMINA-TION.

THIS ONE, THOUGH, SEEMS FAIRLY CASUAL ABOUT IT ALL. THERE ISN'T A HUN-DRED PERCENT GUARANTEE HE CAN COME BACK...

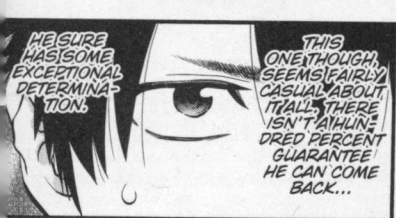

HUMANS ARE USUALLY SO ABNORMALLY FIXATED ON LIVING...

. . . . .

I CAN'T TURN OVER YOUR PILLOW UNLESS YOU'RE ASLEEP.

HUH?

THEN GO TO SLEEP.

right...

Go ahead.

BESIDES, CONSIDERING HOW STRONG HIS SPIRITUAL POWER IS, I SUPPOSE THE CHANCES HE WON'T BE ABLE TO RETURN ARE CLOSE TO ZERO.

FINE.

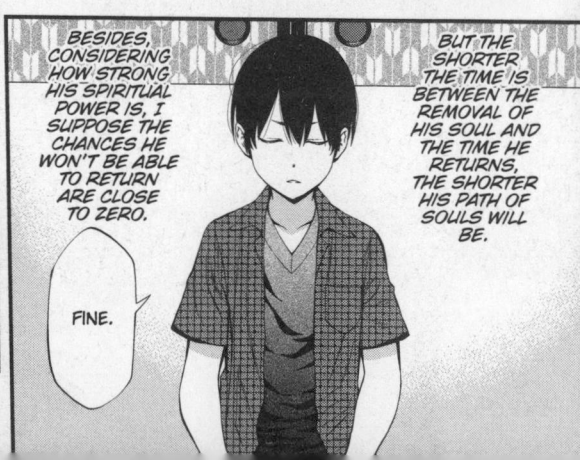

BUT THE SHORTER THE TIME IS BETWEEN THE REMOVAL OF HIS SOUL AND THE TIME HE RETURNS, THE SHORTER HIS PATH OF SOULS WILL BE.

B-BUT... FALLING ASLEEP IN A SITUATION LIKE THIS?
There's no way...
LEAVE IT TO ME, YEP! ♡
HUP!
HIDE AND SEEK
BONK
AUGH!
OH...?
I'LL JUST GIVE YOU ONE WARN-ING...
SHE MUST OPEN THE DOOR TO HER BODY HERSELF.
BECAUSE IF YOU OPEN IT FOR HER...
YOUR SOUL WILL END UP INHABITING HER BODY.
NOW THEN...
OOO...
OOO
SEE YOU LATER!

!!
TH...
THIS IS...
THE PATH OF SOULS!
WAAAAH!
NANAO!
NANAO!!!
DASH
!
ONII-CHAN?!

SHLOOP
SPL-O-O-SH
ARE YOU OKAY, NANAO ?!
ONII-CHANN ...
ぬる―――ん
SLIIIP
UH?
Ah!
GFERBLE! I'M S-SLIP--
Glerb!
GASP! ONII-CHA--
Herp!
DID HE GO THERE TO SAVE HER, OR TO FINISH HER OFF?
I'M NOT SURE...

HAAH! HAAH!
HAAH!
A-ARE YOU OKAY, NANAO?!
HAAH!
HAAH!
YEAH! I'M FINE!
THANK YOU FOR COMING TO SAVE ME...
ONII-CHAN! ♡
BA-THUMP
GASP
Booobies!
WHAT'S WRONG, ONIICHAN?
?
I'M F-FIGHTING AS HER BROTHER! AS HER BROTHER!!
IMPURE!!
I DIDN'T SEE THEM! I DIDN'T SEE ANY BOOBS!!

THEN LET'S KEEP MOVING!
WHAT? YOU WERE CRYING JUST MOMENTS AGO, AND NOW YOU'RE FINE?
And your butt's hanging out.
NOW THAT YOU'RE HERE, I'M NOT SCARED OF ANYTHING!
TEE-HEE! ♪
GRIN ♥

WE HAVE TO CLIMB?
Looks like we have no choice.
Can we even get up there?
......
Whoo...
Wah!
Groan!
So, we grab onto these?
They're not gonna bite us or anything, are they?
Gross!
Sorry.
Huh?! That easily?!
SHLOOP
MOAN
Here we go!
GRAB
H-hey! You're climbing first?!
Catch Nanao if I fall!
Huh?! Uh...
Be sure to watch Nanao, Oniichan!
But...

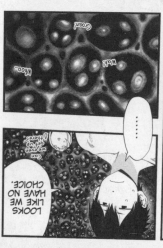

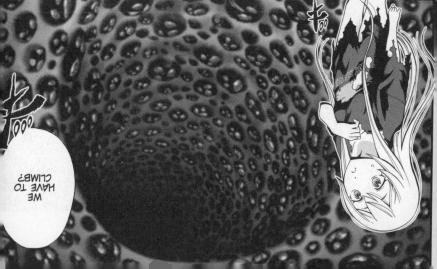

HUP!
HUP!
I...
I CAN'T WATCH THAT!
HUP ...
LICK LICK LICK LICK
FLINCH
EEEEP!
SLIDE
AH!
GLANCE
HUH?

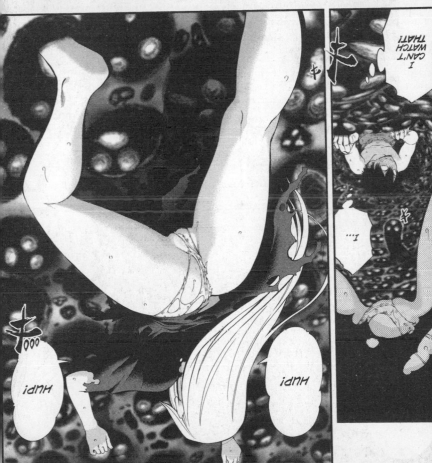

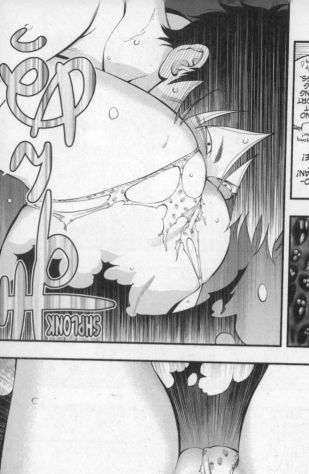

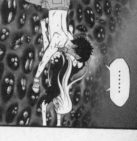

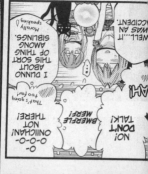

WELL....IT WAS AN ACCIDENT.

...!!

I DUNNO ABOUT THIS SORT OF THING AMONG SIBLINGS.

Morally speaking.

NO! DON'T TALK!

BMEPPLE MEPP!

ONIICHAN! NOT THERE!

O-O-O-O-O-O!

That's going too far!

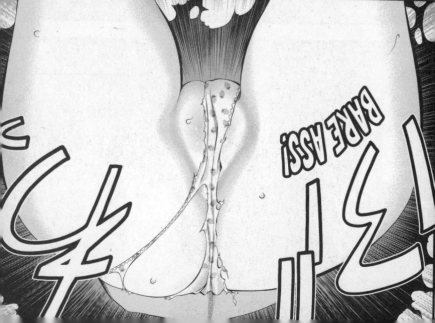

BARE ASS!

SHPLONK

Argh.
HOP HOP
I wonder what's coming next?!
TH- THERE'S MORE?
STAGGER STAGGER
GEE, SHE SURE SEEMS GUTSIER THAN ME DOWN HERE...
SPIN SPIN
MEEP!
MEEP!
SPIN
HEY!!
!

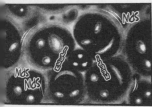

YOU'VE GOT TO BE **NICE** TO EACH OTHER!

ALL YOU BIG ONES CAN'T GANG UP ON THAT LITTLE ONE!

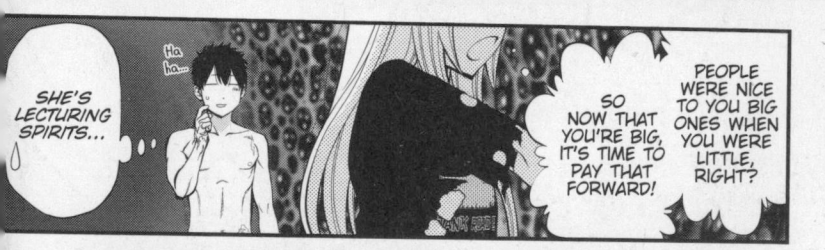

SHE'S LECTURING SPIRITS...

Ha ha...

SO NOW THAT YOU'RE BIG, IT'S TIME TO PAY THAT FORWARD!

PEOPLE WERE NICE TO YOU BIG ONES WHEN YOU WERE LITTLE, RIGHT?

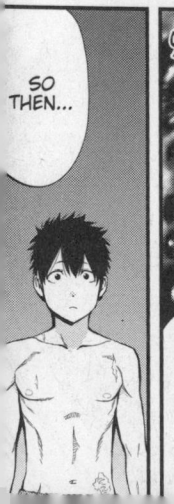

SO THEN...

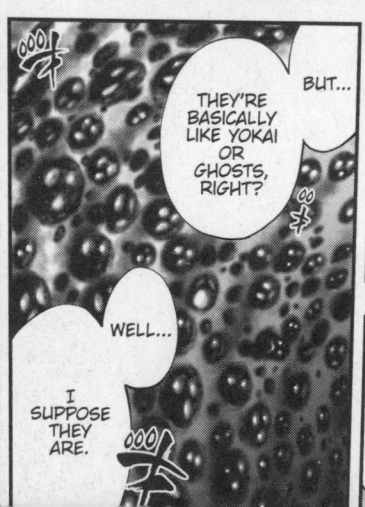

THEY'RE BASICALLY LIKE YOKAI OR GHOSTS, RIGHT?

BUT...

WELL...

I SUPPOSE THEY ARE.

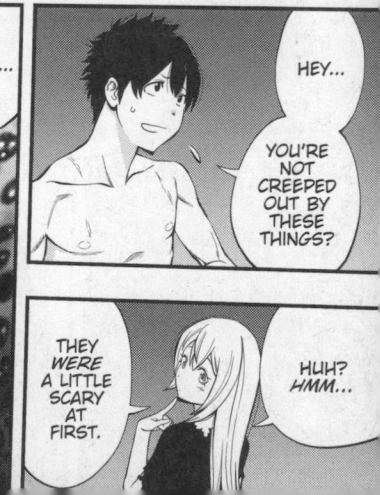

HEY...

YOU'RE NOT CREEPED OUT BY THESE THINGS?

THEY **WERE** A LITTLE SCARY AT FIRST.

HUH? HMM...

THEY'RE JUST LIKE NANAO!
WE'RE FRIENDS! ♪

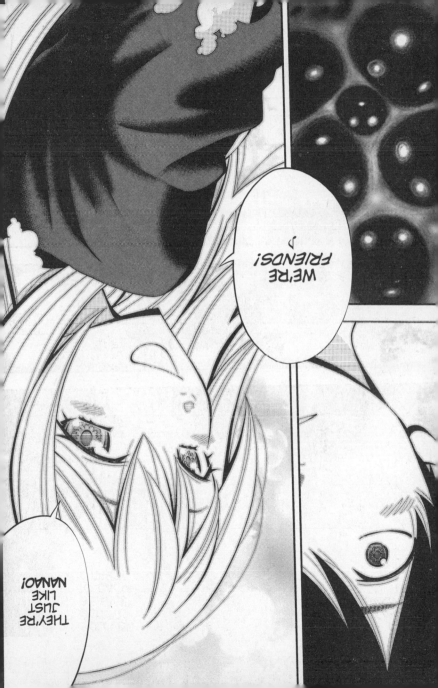

ふわぁぁ
FUWAA
OH!
ふおぅ
FWOO
GLOOW
ぱああっ
OHH!
TANK ROAD!!
WOW!
SO PRETTY!
OH...
MAKURA-GAESHI, RETURN ME TO MY BODY.
YOU'RE DONE?
YEAH.
ICCHAN WAS RIGHT. THIS IS NANAO'S ROAD TO WALK.
I WAS THE ONE WHO NEEDED TO LET HER GO.
NANAO...

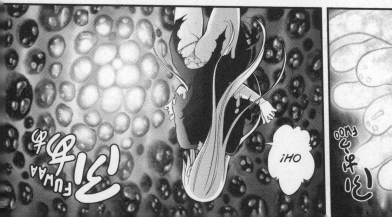

THAT
YOU'D
GROWN
SO
MUCH.

I DIDN'T
EVEN
REALIZE...

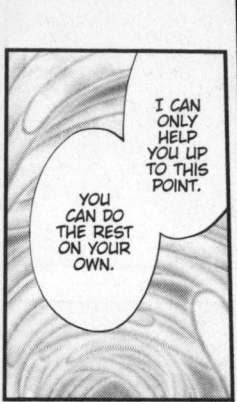

I CAN ONLY HELP YOU UP TO THIS POINT.

YOU CAN DO THE REST ON YOUR OWN.

HUH? WHY?!

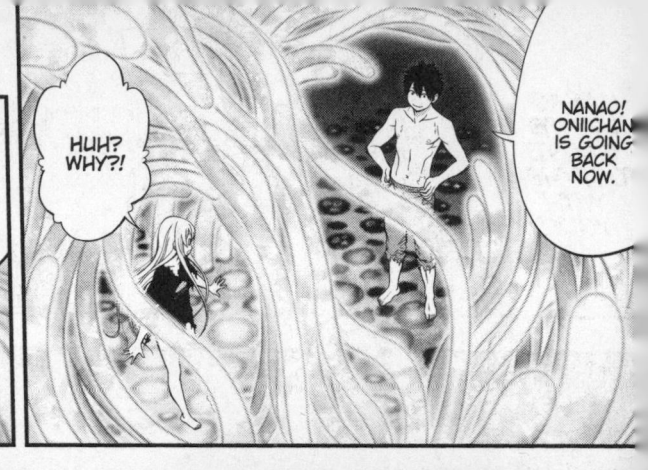

NANAO! ONIICHAN IS GOING BACK NOW.

......

THIS IS *YOUR* TIME TO SHINE!

YOU HAVE TO FINISH THIS TRIAL ON YOUR OWN!

I GOT THIS!

YEAH!

SQUEEZE

FROM HERE!

YOU TAKE IT...

IT'LL BE OKAY! YOU CAN DO IT!!

NANAO WANTS TO LIVE TOGETHER WITH YOU!!

AND GO TO SCHOOL WITH YOU GUYS!

NANAO WANTS TO EAT TOGETHER WITH YOU GUYS...

I'M GETTING BACK TO MY BODY!!

I SWEAR...

ZA...

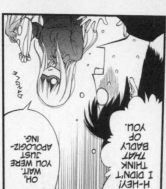
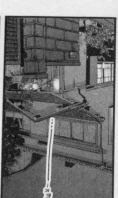
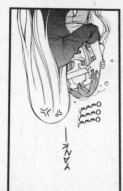
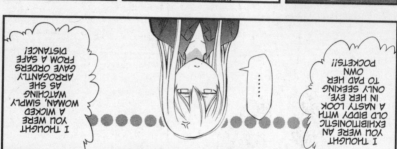
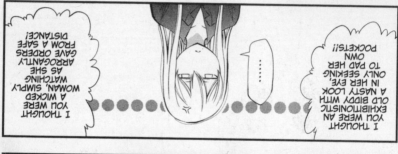
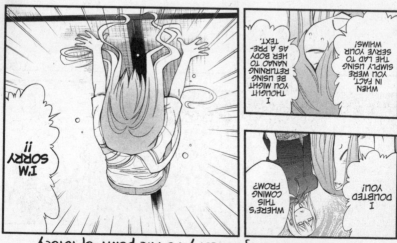

Extra: Witnessing honesty to the point of idiocy

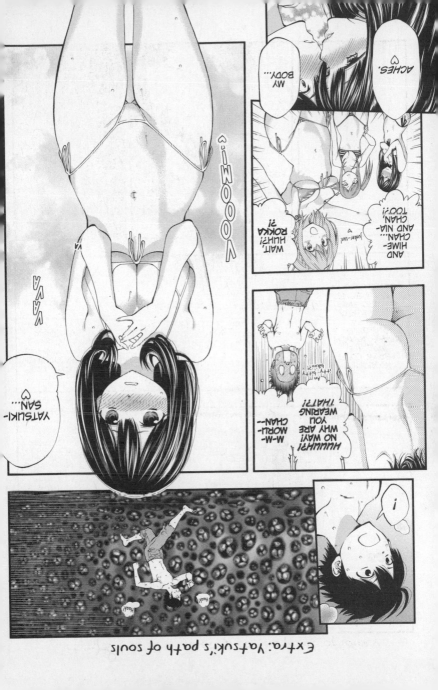

Extra: Yatsuki's path of souls

PLEASE, MAKE IT STOP. ♡
NO! MORU-CHAN WOULDN'T SAY THAT!
YATSUKI... ♡
Time for a real match!
WE CAN'T ... AH! ♡
THIS IS ALL IN MY HEAD! IT'S A TRIAL OF DESIRE! A TRIAL I HAVE TO GO THROUGH TO RETURN TO MY BODY!
JUNKER-SAN, PANYAN-YAN! ♡

THIS IS ULTRA-HARD MODE!!
NOOOO! ♡
AHN!
TWITCH
AH! MM!
TWITCH
AHN!
MAYBE I WOULDN'T MIND STAYING HERE...
FOR-EVER! ♡
AH!

59
Door to the Body...! ♪
HUP...
HAAH!
HUP.
HAAH!
HAAH!
HAAH!
NOM
GRAB
TUUUUG
AH!
SNAP
ブツ
ちっ
HEY!

59
Door to the Body...! ♪
EXPOSED!
NOOO!
YOU JERKS!!
Pervs!

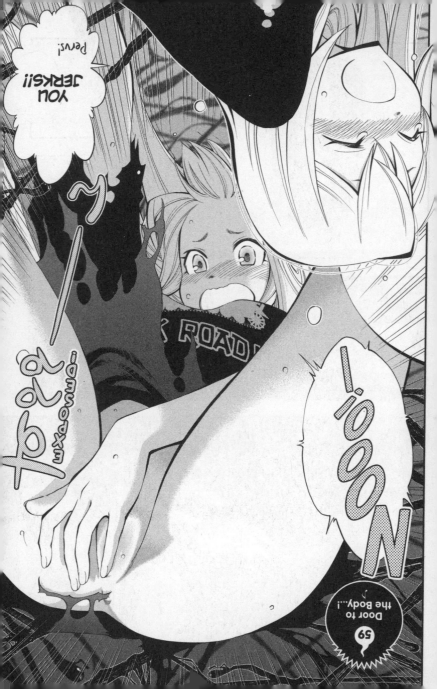

SHA-POP
!
HAAH!
HAAH!
I...
KEE!
KEE!
I GOT THROUGH?
HUH?!

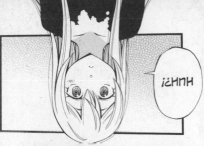

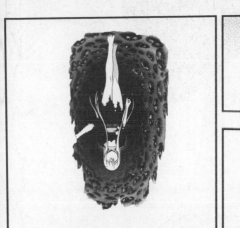

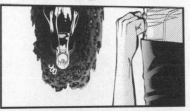

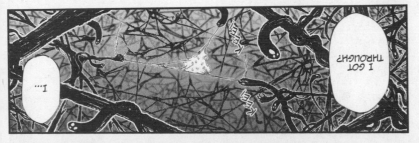

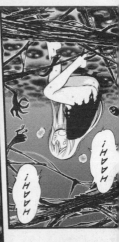

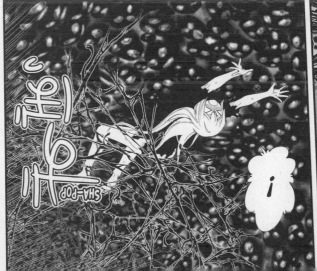

AH!
NANAO
JOLT
OW, OW!
THROB
MY HEAD'S KILLING ME! WHAT THE HELL?!
There's a big lump on it!
HUH?
HUH ?!
HUH ?!
HUH ?!
YOU'RE BACK, JUNKER-SAN?!
HUH ?!
WH-WHAT? I-IS THAT BAD?!
DID THEY SEE ME IN TROU-BLE ?!
THEN WHAT THE HECK IS THIS?!
!

ONIICHAN!

NANAO...

JUNK
SHOP

WHY IS THERE ANOTHER ME?!

HUH ?!

THAT'S NOT RIGHT!

Right?!

BUT I COULDN'T STOP WORRYING, SO I CAME BACK.

DIDN'T YOU GO BACK?

HUH?

I DID.

YOU WERE WORRIED?

WHY WOULDN'T I BE?

JUNK
SHOP

I'VE HAD ENOUGH, YOU KNOW?
HUH...?
SO COULD YOU GO BACK THE WAY YOU CAME AND JUST DIE ALREADY?
WHAT ?!
HOW CAN YOU SAY SUCH A THING, JUNKER-SAN?!
What?!
TH- THAT'S NOT ME!!
THAT'S AWFUL!!
EVEN IF YOU RETURN TO YOUR BODY, YOUR MIND AND BODY WOULDN'T BE IN BALANCE.
THERE'S NO WAY I COULD KEEP ON BABYSITTING YOU LIKE THAT!

WHAT THE HELL IS THAT GUY?!
AND WHY DOES HE LOOK LIKE ME?!
IT'S A REFLECTION OF THE INSECURITIES DEEP WITHIN HER HEART.
?!
"MAYBE THIS IS HOW THE PEOPLE IN MY LIFE REALLY FEEL ABOUT ME...
"MAYBE BEHIND THEIR SMILES, THEY HATE ME, AND WANT ME GONE."
THE SPIRITS HAVE MAGNIFIED THESE VERY, VERY TINY INSECURITIES FROM HER PSYCHE...
AND MADE THEM REAL!
ONII ...
ONIICHAN? WHAT ARE YOU SAYING?

DON'T YOU GET IT? I'M SICK OF YOU. EVEN AFTER ALL THIS TIME, YOUR BODY WON'T EVEN BUDGE.
CRACK
BUT YOU'RE STILL ALIVE, SO I HAVE TO TAKE YOU TO THE HOSPITAL FROM TIME TO TIME, AND THAT COSTS MONEY.
JUNK SHOP
SINCE YOU'RE A SPIRIT, YOU COULD GET ATTACKED BY EVIL GHOSTS AT ANY TIME, AND I HAVE TO PROTECT YOU.
ONII-CHAN?
WHENEVER YOU OPEN YOUR MOUTH, IT'S "PLAY WITH ME, PLAY WITH ME!" IT'S A HUGE PAIN!
YOU CAN'T EVEN TOUCH THINGS! HOW AM I SUPPOSED TO PLAY WITH YOU?!
YOU MUST HAVE HAD ENOUGH. JUST DIE ALREADY! IT'LL MAKE EVERYTHING EASIER!
EVEN ROKKA SAYS SHE'S SICK OF BATHING YOU AND TAKING CARE OF YOU AND STUFF.
I NEVER SAID THAT!! AND I DON'T FEEL THAT WAY!!
I SAID THAT ISN'T ME!!
I KNOW! BUT I HAVE TO VENT MY FRUSTRATION SOMEWHERE!!
YOU'RE SO MEAN, JUNKER-SAN!!
BUT WHY ME?!
BUT... TO THINK THAT IN THE DEPTHS OF NANAO'S HEART...
SHE WAS FEELING ANXIOUS ABOUT THAT.
I COULD GO THERE ONE MORE TIME...
DAMN IT!

NANAO! ONIICHAN DOESN'T THNK THAT WAY!!
AND ROKKA DOESN'T EITHER!!
HE'S A FAKE! HE'S NOT YOUR BIG BROTHER!!
SHE SORT OF KNOWS THAT ALREADY.
BUT THAT'S WHAT SHE'S MOST AFRAID OF: THE WORDS SHE LEAST WANTS TO HEAR FROM THE MOST IMPORTANT PERSON TO HER.
THIS IS THE HARDEST TRIAL!
IF SHE COULD BE CERTAIN THAT IT'S A FAKE...
OR...
CER-TAIN?!
NANAO...
NO...
ONII-CHAN...

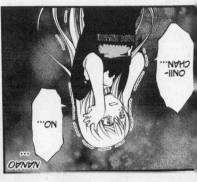

GO ON! GO BACK! JUST DIE
YOU MANAGED TO COME THIS FAR, RIGHT? IT'LL BE EASY!
NO... DON'T SAY THAT.
NO! THAT'S NOT MY BROTHER!
ONIICHAN WOULDN'T SAY SOME-THING LIKE THAT!
ONIICHAN, STOP...
BUT...
GO BACK. DIE.
DIE. GO BACK.
GO BACK GO BACK GO BACK GO BACK GO BACK.
NO.
DIE, DIE, DIE, DIE, DIE, DIE, DIE, DIE!
GO BACK, DIE, GO BACK, DIE, GO BACK, ACK, ACK, ACK, ACK!
STOP --!
!
NO! STOP... STOP!

!!
THAT'S IT!!
IF...
HE'S MY REAL BROTHER ...
DON
TANK ROAD !!
ACK, ACK, ACK...
!
NANAO ?
MY BROTHER WOULD...
YANK
ONIICHAN!! LOOK AT THIS!!

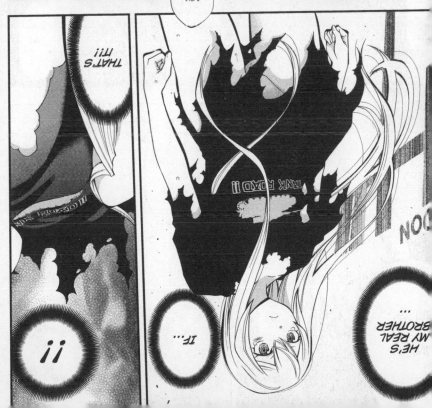

FLASH
ぬど
JUNK
SHOP
NHA?!

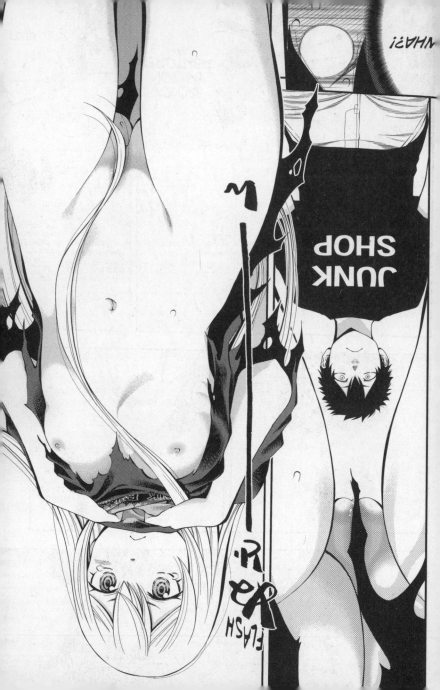

WHAAAT ?!!
PANIC
Ohhh!
......
WHAT ARE YOU TRYING TO DO HERE?
WHAT ... AM I TRYING TO DO?
I KNEW IT! IT ISN'T HIM!
JUNK SHOP
IT'S NOT HIM! IT'S NOT HIM!!
IT'S NOT HIM!!!
YOU'RE NOT MY BROTHER !!!
MY REAL BROTHER IS MORE LIKE AHHHH! AND FREAKS OUT AND LOOKS LIKE THIS!
HE WOULD NEVER BE ALL CALM AND BE LIKE, "WHAT ARE YOU TRYING TO DO HERE?"
AHHHH!
What are you trying to do here?
PLUS...

YOUR WIENER ISN'T STANDING LIKE A ROCKET!!!
HI-DUUUUUN
YOU'RE A FAKE!!
STRIDE STRIDE STRIDE
FAKEY FAKE!!
N- NO...
I'M... NOT A FA--
FAKEY FAKE FAKE-FACE!!
FAKE!!
WRIGGLE WRIGGLE
WRIGGLE
WRIGGLE WRIGGLE

FAAAAKE!!!
BWOOOSH

NICE WORK!

SHE...
HE'S GONE?
DEFEATED THE DARKNESS OF HER HEART!!

......
......
SO. HE LUSTS AFTER HIS LITTLE SISTER?
THAT WAS HER WAY OF DETERMINING IF HE WAS FAKE OR NOT? WHAT THE HELL?
PSST
PSST
HE'LL GO FOR ANYTHING FEMALE, HUH?
Even I'm weirded out here.
PSST
PSST
HE'S A REAL SKEEVY BASTARD!
WAHH!!
NO! YOU'VE GOT IT ALL WRONG! IT'S NOT LIKE I WANT HER... IT'S A PHYSIO-LOGICAL REACTION!
PAT
!
THERE'S A CERTAIN LINE THAT PEOPLE SHOULD NEVER CROSS.
INCEST IS TABOO AMONG MANY WORLD CULTURES, AND IN JAPAN, ILLEGAL AS FAR BACK AS THE ENGI-SHIKI LAWS OF 927...
DON'T USE THAT SERIOUS TONE ON ME!
I said it's not like that!
SOB!
AT ANY RATE, SHE'S OVERCOME HER FINAL TRIAL.
PAT
SOB SOB SOB SOB
SKEEVY BASTARD

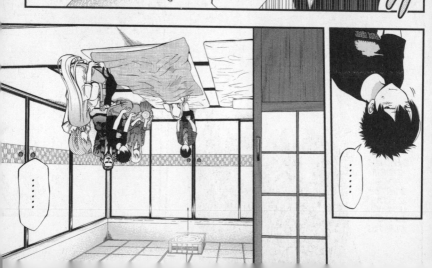

FRANKLY, I DIDN'T EXPECT SUCH A FRAGILE SOUL WOULD GET THIS FAR.
CON-GRAT-ULA-TIONS!
NOW SHE JUST HAS TO OPEN THE DOOR TO HER BODY!
C'MON...
NANAO!
GET BACK...
TANK ROAD!!
TUP...
TO YOUR BODY!!
HUH?

THIS IS...
BAAAAN
THE DOOR TO MY BODY?!

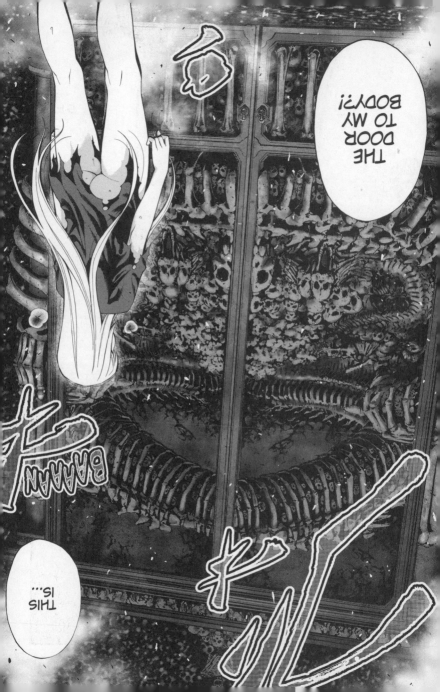

HUH?
WHAT?
HEY...
HOLD ON A MINUTE!
JUST WHAT...
IS THAT?!
60
Faint Light...! ♪
THIS IS...

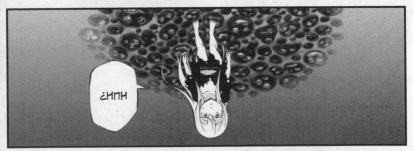

THE DOOR TO MY BODY?!
ゴゴ
オオ

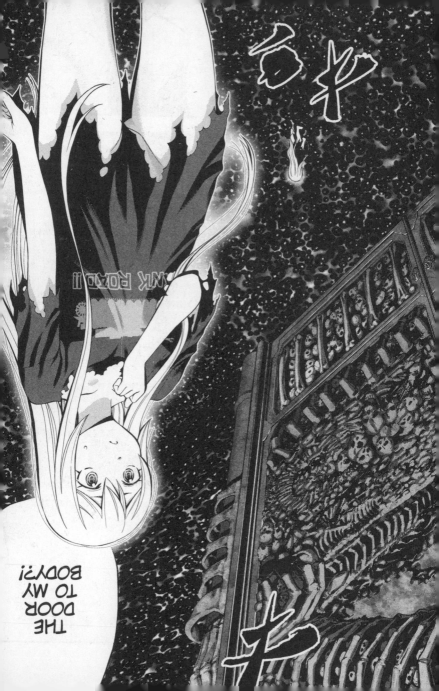

BAAAAN
60
Faint Light...! ♪
SO BIG! TOO BIG!
'TIS...
......
FROM THE BEGINNING, I HAD THE FEELING THAT SOMETHING WAS OFF.
I'D NOTICED THE PRESENCE OF SOME MYSTERIOUS DISTORTION...
BETWEEN HER BODY AND SPIRIT.
BUT I DIDN'T EXPECT IT TO LOOK LIKE THIS.
CAN NANAO OPEN THAT ALL BY HERSELF?

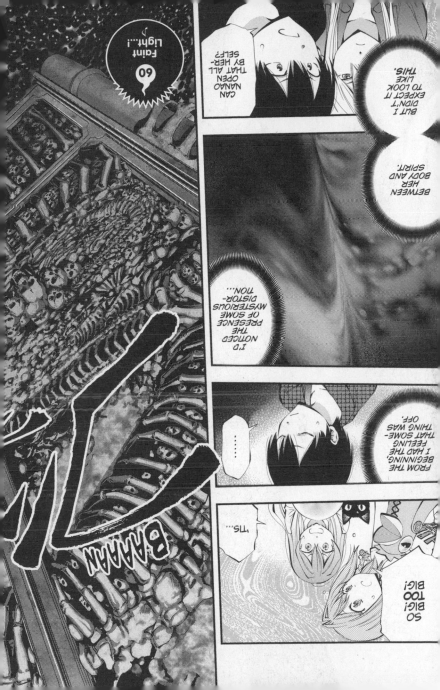

......
WELL...
HN!
PUSHHH
HNGHHH!
HRNGH!
GRRRR~!!
YANK YANK
YAAAANK
BANG
......
BANG BANG
BANG
......
I HIGHLY DOUBT IT.
GLOOOM...

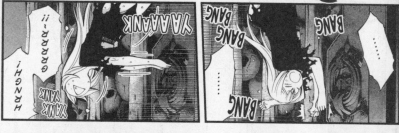

HIC...
SOB...

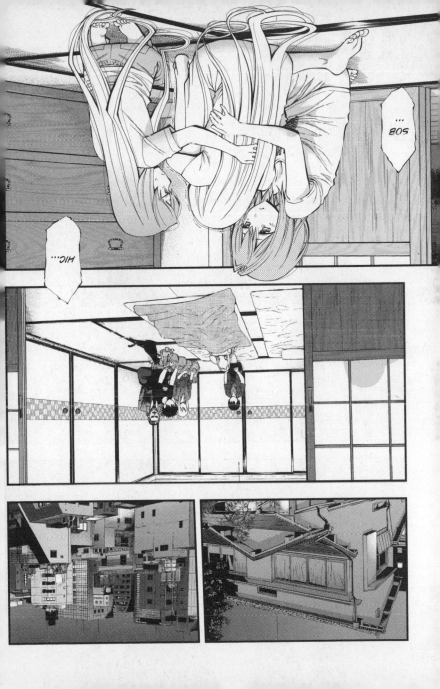

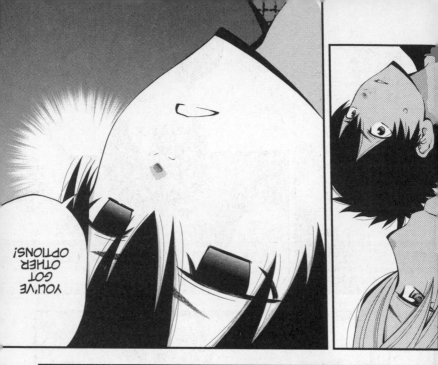

YOU'VE GOT OTHER OPTIONS!

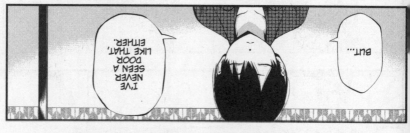

I'VE NEVER SEEN A DOOR LIKE THAT, EITHER.

....BUT.

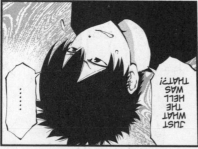

......

JUST WHAT THE HELL WAS THAT?!

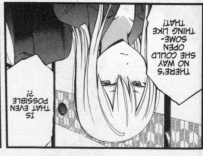

IS THAT EVEN POSSIBLE?!

THERE'S NO WAY SHE COULD OPEN SOME-THING LIKE THAT!

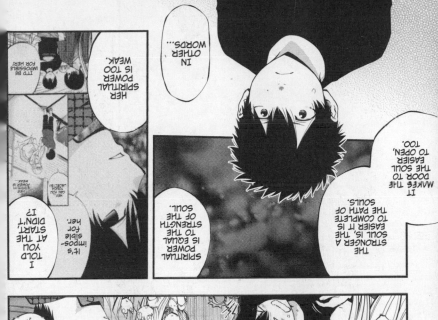

IN OTHER WORDS....

HER SPIRITUAL POWER IS TOO WEAK.

IT'D BE IMPOSSIBLE FOR HER!

HEY, CAN YOU START? IT'S WEAK...

I TOLD YOU AT THE START, DIDN'T I?

It's impossible for her.

SPIRITUAL POWER IS EQUAL TO THE STRENGTH OF THE SOUL.

THE STRONGER A SOUL IS, THE EASIER IT IS TO COMPLETE THE PATH OF SOULS.

IT MAKES THE DOOR TO THE SOUL EASIER TO OPEN, TOO.

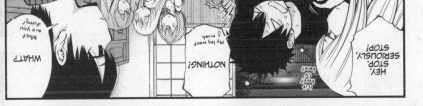

HEY, STOP, SERIOUSLY, STOP!

My leg went numb.

NOTHING!

What are you doing?

WHAT?

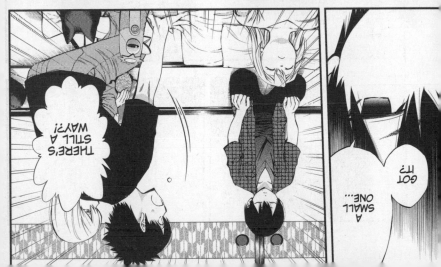

GOT IT?

A SMALL ONE...

THERE'S STILL A WAY?!

ETHEREAL ENERGY!
YOU MEAN TO GATHER SHOCKERGY!
GATHER SHOCK-ERGY?!
YES, SHOCKERGY IS FEAR PLUS ETHEREAL ENERGY.
WE YOKAI LIVE LONG BY OBTAINING IT...
AND WE CAN ALSO STRENGTHEN OURSELVES BY ABSORB-ING GREAT QUANTITIES OF IT.
SO THEN IF NANAO COULD GATHER SHOCK-ERGY TOO, THEN ...
'TIS A SKILL ONLY US YOKAI POSSESS.
A MERE SOUL LIKE NANAO CANNOT DO IT.
BUT ...
THEN HOW...?
THIS IS WHERE I COME IN.
SOME TIME IS NECESSITATED FOR A YOKAI TO ABSORB AND ASSIMI-LATE...
THE ETHE-REAL ENERGY THEY HAVE GATH-ERED.

AT A POINT BEFORE IT'S COMPLETELY ASSIMILAT-ED...
I CAN WITHDRAW IT AND TRANSFER IT TO HER.
I AM A YOKAI WHO EXTRACTS SOULS, YOU KNOW.
YOU CAN DO THAT?!
SO THEN ...!
IF WE GO AROUND GATHERING TONS OF IT...!!
JUST SO YOU KNOW, NO MATTER HOW MUCH YOU STARTLE HUMANS, THAT'S NO GOOD...
SINCE YOU CAN'T GATHER MUCH FROM THEM.
It'd have to be in the tens of thousands.
......
SO THEN... YOKAI?
A-ARE THERE ANY YOKAI WHO ARE SCARED OF US?
HMMM ...
!
THERE ARE! BIG ONES!

HIME-CHAN!
THAT ARM OF YOURS, YATSUKI...
WILL SCARE MOST YOKAI.
AND YOU CAN ABSORB ETHEREAL ENERGY, TOO.
I MEAN, YOU ABSORBED IT FROM ME!
IT'S HUMILIATING, BUT IT'S BEST FOR NOW IF I JUST WITHDRAW ...!!
THE POWER IS SEEPING OUT OF ME...!!
I'M FEELING FEAR?!
HEY!
STOP!
ETHE-REAL FUSION ...
WITH THAT ARM!!

......
ABOUT HOW MANY?
HM?
FIRST, I'D WANT YOU TO GATHER ENOUGH TO GET HER TO THE POINT WHERE SHE CAN TOUCH THINGS.
THIS IS JUST MY GUESS, BUT...
ABOUT THREE TO FIVE AS POWERFUL AS THAT NEKOMATA-CHAN OVER THERE.
OR ABOUT TWELVE TO FIFTEEN LIKE THAT MINI-GRANDMA OVER THERE, I GUESS?
HOP
WHO ARE YOU CALLING A MINI-GRAND-MA?!
IT'D BE ABOUT A HUNDRED OF YOU.
WHY?! I'M NOT THAT WEAK!!
SPROING
Oh, so you're a rokurokubi.
TWO OF MY LEVEL IS ABOUT ENOUGH!
TWO WOULD ONLY GATHER YOU A BIT OF SNOT.
WHO ARE YOU CALLING SNOT?!
I CAN SEE THE LIGHT.
IT'S A REALLY TINY, FAINT LIGHT...
BUT IT'S A DEFINITE LIGHT OF HOPE!
WAIT JUST A BIT LONGER, NANAO!

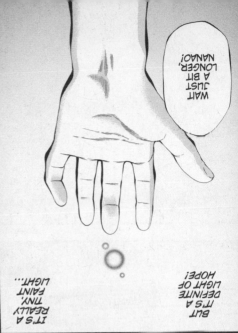

TEN OR TWENTY IS A PIECE OF CAKE!
I SWEAR...
I'M GONNA GET YOU BACK TO YOUR BODY!!
I SWEAR...
CLENCH
I'M GONNA GRAB HOLD OF THAT LIGHT!!

I SWEAR!!
YOU WANT TO KNOW THE DIFFERENCE BETWEEN SPIRITUAL ENERGY AND YOKAI ENERGY?
THAT'S RIGHT.
THEY'RE THE SAME THING!
THERE'S NOTHING DIFFERENT ABOUT THEM ASIDE FROM THEIR NAMES.
THE ETHEREAL ENERGY OF HUMANS--WHAT WE COMMONLY CALL PSYCHIC POWER--IS SPIRITUAL ENERGY.
THE ETHEREAL ENERGY OF YOKAI IS YOKAI ENERGY.
THAT'S WHY WHEN YOU USE THE DETECTOR, YOU CAN'T TELL IF IT'S A YOKAI OR A PSYCHIC.

ARE YOU WONDERING ABOUT THE YOUNG MAN WHO DEFEATED YUKIMURA-KUN?
YES...
WHAT WAS THE RESULT OF YOUR NE ADJUDICATION?
HE'S LEVEL ONE.
LEVEL ONE...
SO IT'S A LESS THAN 10% POSSIBILITY THAT HE'S AN NE.
HE'S QUITE THE POWERFUL PSYCHIC, ISN'T HE?
Ha ha!
A PSYCHIC?!
THERE'S NO WAY!!
DON'T "HA HA!" ME! HE'S AS SHIFTY AS ALWAYS.
TP
TP
TP
EVEN THE MOST POWERFUL PSYCHIC WOULD BE D OR C CLASS AT BEST...
THERE'S NO WAY...
THIS IS A-CLASS. NO. THIS IS...S-CLASS LEVEL!!
PANT...
SHAAA
THAT BOY COULD BE JUST HUMAN!!
BIING
!
Additional report
Houjou Sakurako-sama
I'm contacting you to inform you that we've completed the additional investigation into Nishizuru Yatsuki.
I've attached a report with the details.
Please take a look.
HEY!
!

GRAB
URK!
SLAM
......
GAH ...
AGH ...
WHY ...?
NGH.
YOU... YOU'RE ...!

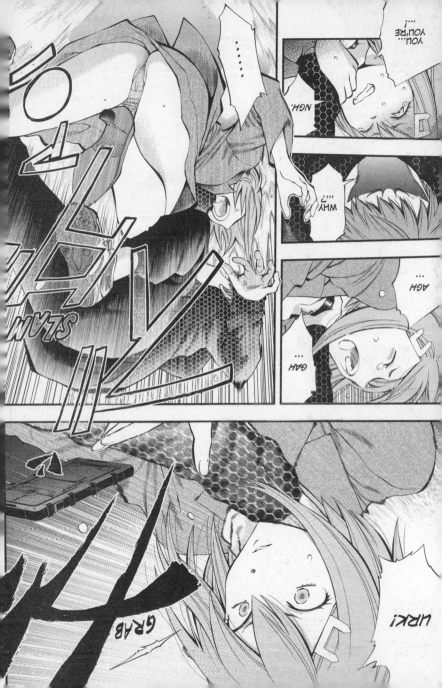

KIZUKI-KUN!
WHY DID YOU LET YUKIMURA-SAN GO ALONE?!
HE WASN'T... I WAS...
YOU THINK SOMEONE LIKE YOU CAN BE YUKIMURA-SAN'S PARTNER ?!
NGH! I FORGOT... THIS KID IS YUKI-MURA-KUN'S...
Y-YOU THINK YOU CAN... GET AWAY WITH DOING THIS?
!
SO, IT'S THESE GUYS?
HEY! DON'T JUST...
AGH!
THEY'RE NOTHING BUT SMALL FRY!
THESE GUYS GOT THE JUMP ON YUKIMURA-SAN?!

!
......
I'M GONNA GET THESE GUYS.
HEY...
!
SHIVER
I'VE FINALLY FOUND HER!

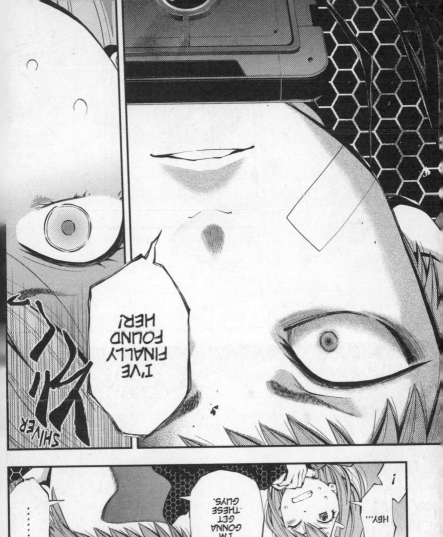

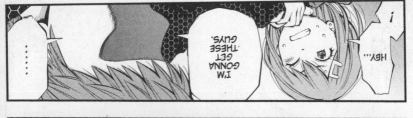

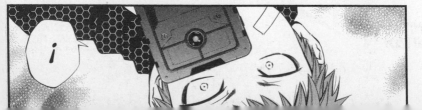

NAME
Makabe Ichie
CLASS
D
TYPE
Nurikabe (assumed)
MAKABE ICHIE!!
Skeevy bas-tard?
SKEEVY BASTARD
Bye.
Icchaan-!
Stay back, you obnoxious cow!
GRIND
Yokai Girls 6 End

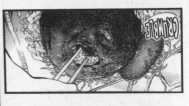
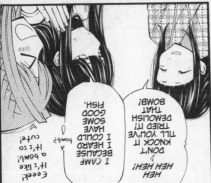
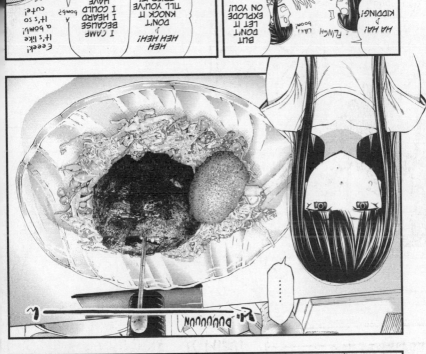
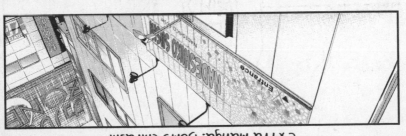

Extra manga: Bomb chirashi!

THERE IT IS!!
PAAAAN!
ぱぁあぁーーん!
MMM! IT'S SO GOOD!!
THE FISH IS SOFT AND FRESH, AND IT GETS TOP MARKS FOR VOLUME!!
HEE!
EHEE
THE FLAVOR EXPLODES IN YOUR MOUTH, JUST LIKE THE NAME SUGGESTS!!
RIGHT, NIA-CHAN?
PLIP
PLIP
PLIP
HUH? WAIT...
Are you crying?!
IT'S OKAY! SHE'S JUST SAYING IT'S GOOD!
NADESHIKO
NADESHICO-SUSHI.
AKIHABARA CRANE LAB
I-IS SHE? OKAY, THEN...
Wait, when did those cat ears show up?

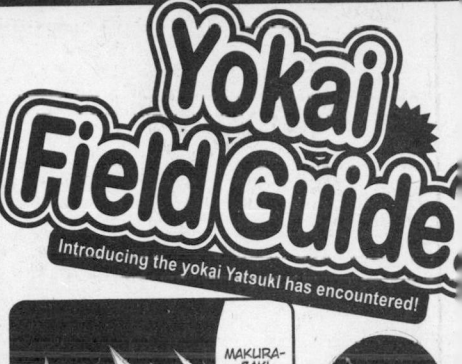

Yokai Field Guide

Introducing the yokai Yatsuki has encountered!

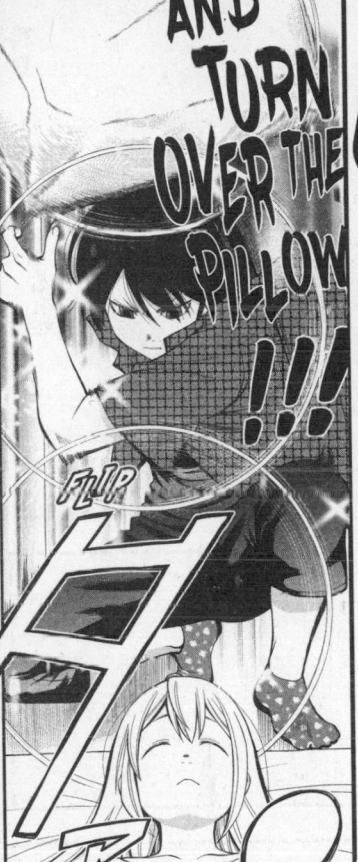

AND TURN OVER THE PILLOW!!!

FLIP

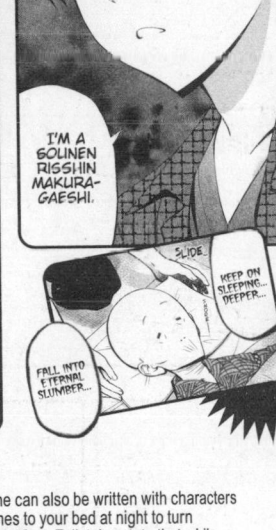

MAKURA-ZAKI RISAI...

I'M A SOUKEN RISSHIN MAKURA-GAESHI.

SLIDE

KEEP ON SLEEPING... DEEPER...

FALL INTO ETERNAL SLUMBER...

This yokai appears in stories across Japan. Its name can also be written with characters that mean "anti-pillow." This mischievous yokai comes to your bed at night to turn your pillow over or swap the position of your head and feet. Folk tales state that while dreaming, the soul leaves the body, so if the pillow is turned over during that time, the soul won't be able to return to the body.

Placing a dead body with its head facing north is also called "makuragaeshi" because of the idea that there is a change in pillow position between the world of human life and the world of death.

Makuragaeshi are said to look like children, but Toriyama Sekien's *Gazu Hyakki Yakou* features a frightening version who steals human lives and is drawn to resemble the Nio.

First Appearance: Chapter 56

枕返し

(TURNER OF PILLOWS)

MAKURAGAE:

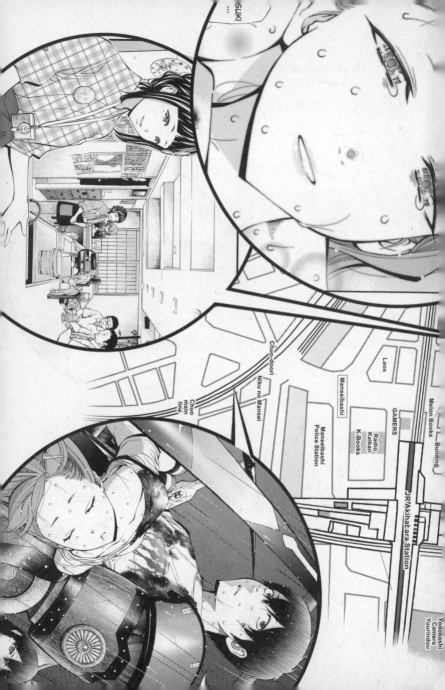

Laox

Manseibashi

Chuo-doori

Niku no Mansei

Chuo
main
line

Manseibashi
Police Station

Radio
Kaikan

GAMERS

K-Books

Melon Books

Building

JR/Akihabara Station

Yodobashi
Camera
Yuurinidou

YOKAI GIRLS
AKIBA MAP
N
W
E
S
Soto-kanda 5-chome
Kiyomizu Zakashita
Kuramaebashi-docri
Kanda Myoujin
Sankou Rare Item Shop
Maid Cafe Pinafore Third Branch
452
Animate
Torano Ana Flagship Flagship Shop A
437
Sofmap
Nadeshiko Sushi
YA...

SEVEN SEAS' GHOST SHIP PRESENTS

YOKAI GIRLS

story and art by KAZUKI FUNATSU

VOL.6

TRANSLATION
Jennifer Ward

ADAPTATION
Bambi Eloriaga-Amago

LETTERING AND LAYOUT
Phil Christie

COVER DESIGN
Nicky Lim

PROOFREADER
Janet Houck
Stephanie Cohen

EDITOR
Shannon Fay

PRODUCTION ASSISTANT
CK Russell

PRODUCTION MANAGER
Lissa Pattillo

EDITOR-IN-CHIEF
Adam Arnold

PUBLISHER
Jason De

YOKAI SHOJO-MONSTER GIRL VOL. 6
© 2014 Kazuki Funatsu
All rights reserved.
First published in 2014 by SHUEISHA Inc. Tokyo.
English translation rights arranged by SHUEISHA Inc.
through TOHAN CORPORATION, Tokyo.

ISBN: 978-1-947804-24-1

Printed in Canada

First Printing: January 2019

10 9 8 7 6 5 4 3 2 1

FOLLOW US

READING DIRECTIONS

This book reads from **right to left**, Japanese style.
If this is your first time reading manga, you start
reading from the top right panel on each page and
take it from there. If you get lost, just follow the
numbered diagram here. It may seem backwards at
first, but you'll get the hang of it! Have fun!!

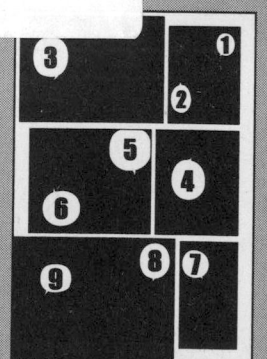